AND SO IT IS

ESSAYS ON THE SPIRITUAL LIFE

BY REVEREND JAMES FOX

PM LIBRARY

Most of these essays were published in The Madera Tribune over a period of about four years. The newspaper continues to publish Jim Fox's work on Fridays.
—Chuck Doud, Editor and Publisher, Madera Tribune, Madera, California.

ISBN: 978-0-9824276-5-1

PM Library
an imprint of Poetic Matrix Press
www.poeticmatrixpress.com

PREFACE

And So It Is is based on the author's life experiences both before and after becoming a Religious Science Minister. Practical spirituality is magnificently illustrated in the one hundred spiritual essays contained in this book. These essays are inspirational; they are also clear instructions for successful living based on the principles taught in the Science of Mind.

Reading these spiritual essays may encourage the reader to:

- Look more deeply into the patterns of nature and apply them to their daily activities.
- Recognize the Creative Force of the Universe (Spirit or God) in every being.
- Become more aware of the Power of Love.
- Make the choice to take charge of their life.
- Release thoughts of lack, worry and fear.
- Experience love, harmony, joy, abundant living and peace of mind.

These essays were originally written as a weekly column in the Madera Tribune Newspaper. Several readers of these articles in the Madera Tribune have commented to Reverend Jim that after reading the articles they have a better or clearer understanding as to what Religious Science is and how it can be applied to everyday activities. One even made the remark, "so, your church does believe in God."

When meeting Reverend Jim in public places, readers have thanked him for his articles; "...I look forward to reading them every Friday." Others have called and made comments that his articles really helped them with problems they were having, or that they now see things from a different perspective.

There are valuable lessons in these spiritual essays written in simple, straight forward language that everyone can understand. Read *And So It Is* for yourself and enjoy the journey.

About the Front Cover

The title, *And So It Is*, is the ending of the 5 or 7 step affirmative prayer that is used in the Science of Mind teaching. The Science of Mind teaching relates to what Jesus taught and that was, "it is done unto you as you believe." When closing the affirmative prayer we use *And So It Is* which means: it is done, I accept, I believe, I know, then the prayer is released to God to act on the request.

The earth on the front cover is to remind us that it is all complete with everything man needs at the time of Creation. The discoveries man makes are the unfolding of what is already there.

In Genesis 1:9 "...God said, let the waters that are under the sky be gathered together in one place, and let the dry land appear; and it was so." In Genesis 1:10 "...God called the dry land Earth; and the gathering together of the waters He called Seas; and God saw that it was good."

Contents

Dedication

This book is dedicated to the people who were the inspiration for me spending the time and effort to complete this work; the people who were always there with support and love when I didn't feel like continuing.

First is my beautiful wife Joanna who kept her support strong and encouraged me to continue each week. Second is Annette Nordine who kept pushing me to get started and would not take no for an answer. Third is Reverend Marcia Pearce who was my first teacher in the Science of Mind teaching and was always there for me when I had questions about my spiritual development. Fourth is all the members of our church who make me feel good with their comments about the articles each week; and to all who call with their comments about the articles and encourage me to keep writing because they get so much help from reading these weekly articles in the Madera Tribune.

AND SO IT IS

Introduction

There are a great many people faced with challenges, large and small, that are looking for a way to meet them or eliminate them from their lives completely. Through many challenges, with hard work, embarrassment, and resentment I made a promise to myself to learn from my challenges and not repeat them. Sometimes we get ourselves backed into a corner and the only way out is to move forward. When one is in a corner, with one's back to the wall, you can't go left or you can't go right, the only way out of the corner is to move forward.

During my lifetime, I have been presented with these kinds of situations and was able to solve them to my own satisfaction. I tried to live my life by the Golden Rule. Sometimes the challenges were a hardship on me because I didn't want to involve anyone else in a situation I had created myself.

There are those who point fingers and place blame on others just to make themselves look good in the eyes of those they want to impress. I could never do that to anyone because if it was my mistake, I always felt better "fessing up" to it and not allowing it to happen again.

The life I lived, after getting out of the military in 1954, had its highs and lows, but I was able to get above the lows and look forward to the highs to keep pace with everything going on around me. It seemed like life was a struggle and there was conflict always adding to that struggle.

I moved from Ohio to California in 1979 and found the Science of Mind teaching in 1986. My life did a 180 degree turn because I found out I could control the challenges in my life by changing the way I was thinking. People create everything in their life by the way they think and the action they take on those thoughts.

The Science of Mind is not about mind control; it is about knowing that the Creative Force of the Universe (God) is the source of all our good and this loving God dwells at the very center of our being. It is what Jesus referred to as the Father within, Ralph Waldo Emerson referred to it as the Over Soul. I know I can use this Creative Force anytime for any reason. I live my life now in balance with mind, body and Spirit and the challenges are much easier to overcome and replace with the joy of life.

Dr. Ernest Holmes, in his book Seminar Lectures describes our teaching: "We are a group of people who believe in a truth, which we are endeavoring to prove. What is it? It is that God is all there is, not up in the sky, but right here. God is the mountain. Whatever the thing is we call God, there is only That and nothing else from which all is made. When we awake, we shall be like God, but we shall have to see God as God is, and not as you and I think God ought to be."

Dr. Holmes also writes: "The philosophy of Religious Science is nothing new to the world. It is rather a synthesis of the greatest concepts which have ever come to the mind of man. The law of Moses, the love of Christ, the ethics of Buddha, the morals of Confucius, the deep spiritual revelations of the saints of the Middle Ages, the laws of parallels and compensation of Emerson, the logic of Kant, the spirituality of Swedenborg, the beauty of Browning, and the wide, universal sweep of Walt Whitman all find an exalted place in the philosophy of Religious Science."

The short essays in this book will be of help to those who are looking for affirmations or words of kindness to use in their own thoughts to help overcome different challenges that appear in their daily lives. Enjoy the essays in a way that will create the joy and peace we were created to experience. I see the joy and peace being exercised for all the peoples of the world and the Creative Intelligence of the Universe (God) is always there as a partner in time of need. We can never be alone once we recognize that the indwelling presence of Spirit is there and all we have to do is trust and ask.

Reverend Jim, 2009

MOVE FORWARD WITH CAUTION

There is a place in us which lies open to the Infinite: but when the Spirit brings its gift, by pouring Itself through us, It can give us only what we take. Ernest Holmes, <u>Science of Mind,</u> pg. 151

There are times when opportunity raises its head and we see the potential in it, but then we move too fast and find ourselves in a position of not knowing in which direction to turn. Everyone wants to move forward to better themselves to a life of joy and peace without a lot of hard work.

To provide for our families, one has to work at something in order to receive the items needed that can create a happy life for everyone in the experience. I know in some families it requires the income of two people to support the life style the family wants. That is fine in most cases because the family spends time together and is happy.

There are those looking for something bigger and better without doing the hard work involved. They act so fast that they don't think of what it takes to reach the goal they set for themselves. Moving too fast on a project can get one in trouble because they do not take time to check things out.

I learned a good lesson a few years back that opened my eyes to the fact that the time spent checking things out can steer one out of trouble ahead. My brother and I were invited by my sister's children in Gadsden, Alabama to a surprise birthday party for my sister, who was turning eighty years young. We landed in Birmingham in a down pour of rain and picked up our luggage and then rented a car for the trip from Birmingham to Gadsden.

The car we rented was in a parking garage joined to the air terminal with a sheltered walkway. The rain was coming down very hard all the time we were renting the car and walking to the parking garage.

After putting our luggage in the trunk of the rental car, we were ready to make the trip.

Pulling out of the parking garage onto a street with six lanes of traffic moving very fast and in a down pour of rain was not a good experience.

After getting in the traffic I looked for the windshield wipers and couldn't find the switch. It was a compact foreign car that I was not familiar with and in fast moving traffic with no wipers it was a pretty scary experience. I finally found a place to pull out of the traffic and stop only to get more frustrated looking for the wiper switch. This experience taught me a lesson that I use to this day when attempting something new.

When there is something unfamiliar that I need directions on I rely on the Creative Intelligence of the Universe (God) to give me the wisdom needed to overcome the fear of not knowing what to do. It only takes a few minutes to figure it out once I release the fear and ask God to show me the way.

As Ernest Holmes says, "there is a place in us which lies open to the Infinite" (God), which we should use when asking for help with anything we wish to achieve. Had I taken a couple of minutes looking for the wiper switch, I would not have experienced the fear I had when I was in the down pour and heavy traffic. Everyone should take those few minutes to gain the wisdom to overcome any fear by letting go and letting God help.

And So It Is

Nature Is Always Creating

And ye shall know the truth,
and the truth shall set you free. John 8:32

I was reviewing a book about the wonderful ingenuity of nature written by Samuel Alibrando titled <u>Nature Never Stops Talking</u>. It consisted of several short stories about how the laws of nature work from the smallest of atoms to the size and characteristics of the largest animal known to modern day man, the blue whale.

It was very interesting how the cells of a living organism function with its own intelligence to do a specific job in order to create the five senses in all animals. The intelligence in the cell is the atoms which are one thousand times smaller than the cell and are compared to a complete solar system within each cell. The nucleus is the center of the atom with the electrons orbiting around the nucleus just like the planets orbit around the sun in what man recognizes as our solar system. There was a lot more detail about the atom but that gives us some idea how the intelligence works.

The largest known animal is the blue whale with a heart that can weigh up to one thousand pounds and circulates fourteen thousand pounds of blood through a body that can weigh as much as one hundred ninety tons. The largest dinosaur found to date weighs in at fifty tons which is about one third the size of a blue whale. The difference in size of smallest to the largest is so great, yet both were created out of One Intelligence (God) that is everywhere present and is always creating.

The ever expanding Intelligence never stops creating and is always at work in all forms of nature. The one and only power in the Universe is a power greater than we are but we can use that power in our everyday lives to create a life of peace and harmony for ourselves.

Man is the most intelligent

animal on this planet and is able to make choices as to how to use this power to bring to him a life of abundance. The other animals do what they are supposed to do because their intelligence is installed in them at the time of their creation. Man is finding out his true nature by using this Creative Power in the Universe (God) to guide and direct the action taken on thoughts coming to him from this greater power.

Man is the only animal that recognizes this greater power and to different cultures it means different things and is thought of in different ways. Regardless of how or what one thinks about this greater power, it is the recognition of it that make the difference. People don't think the same way about this greater power because of their belief in what they were taught. Any belief is all right as long as it satisfies the Soul and a person doesn't live their life in fear. When one can see this greater power (God) as love and joy, then they are see-ing the true nature of who they are and that truth will set one free.

And So It Is

My Amazing Physical Body

Know ye not that your body is the temple of the Holy Ghost which is in you, which ye have of God. 1 Corinthians 6:19

The reaction of your body to the different situations we put ourselves in is something of a miracle. The pain we get when we put ourselves in the wrong position is a warning to not do that any more. Our physical body is so constructed that each part of it is given a certain job to do in order for the whole thing to function in unity.

I know our body is created to function in perfect harmony with the Spirit that dwells within it. This Spirit, that dwells within, is the guidance for our life and keeps us in balance with mind, body and spirit.

The mind is the key factor in the operation of the body because of the conscious thoughts we get and the actions we take. The subconscious mind keeps all the vital parts of the body operating without the conscious mind having to think about when to breathe, when your heart beats, when to blink your eyes, and when to swallow. All the functions of the body seem to be automatic and as long as the body is cared for with the right nourishment and liquids, there should never be any problem with health as long as the mind stays balanced with the Spirit that dwells within.

Studies show that when a person receives something of need, the serotonin level in the body increases and that boosts the immune system to a higher level to ward off diseases and other problems. The study shows that the giver had even a higher level of serotonin in their body, and the bystander who saw the exchange had an even higher level of serotonin.

The body we have is such a complex instrument that it cannot be duplicated by man regardless of how intelligent the human being becomes. Man can repair the body with artificial metal joints but will never be able to create muscle, bone joints, tissue, or the lubricant for the joints.

All life on this planet is here now because of the Creative Force of the Universe (God). The oneness of all life is very visible and understandable when you think about the parts of all animals, including man, that are all the same such as, hearts, lungs, kidneys, stomach, intestines, muscle, blood and teeth.

All the animals were created to be what they are and do what they do. Man did not evolve from a monkey because if he had, there would be no more monkeys. Man was created to be a man and a monkey was created to be a monkey just as a raccoon was created to be a raccoon. Man was created with the Spirit of God in the center of his being and that allows God to live life through man as man.

My amazing physical body is a very complex instrument of God and can sustain itself in so many ways because of the chemicals the body can manufacture from the food that is put into it. With my body being the temple of the Holy Spirit, I know I never can be separated from Spirit   because I am Spirit in action.

With God in me as me, I know all I have to do is call on God for guidance and I get the guidance when I get quiet and listen to that small still voice from within. The action I take is always for my best and highest good and always brings to me the love, peace, power, beauty and joy that life is all about. I give thanks for my amazing body.

And So It Is

A Time To Seek and Understand

Every man shall eat and drink and enjoy the good of his labor, it is a gift of God. Ecclesiastes: 3:13

It is so great to see an internationally known person recognizing that people can control their own life by just changing the way they think. A few months ago Oprah Winfrey was telling her story about <u>The Secret</u> and how one could better their life by just recognizing that the Creative Energy of the Universe will respond to the intention one puts in mind and focuses his or her thoughts on. Now she is doing a world wide workshop on the book <u>The New Earth</u> by Eric Tolle.

<u>The New Earth</u> is about the New Thought movement that is spreading world wide and is helping many people understand what the great teacher Jesus was trying to get people to understand. Praying with an affirmative prayer and not a begging prayer was the prayer that Jesus taught. "Pray knowing it is done to you as you believe," is what starts the Creative Energy of the Universe into action. It brings into action what one has set and keeps his or her intention on; keeping that intention at the forefront of one's mind.

The Science of Mind teaching is based on that philosophy; that teaching was introduced in the early part of the last century. We call it New Thought, but is not new because it started with the teachings of Jesus. Change your thinking and you can change the things in your life to bring about more peace, joy and love.

The workshop Oprah is doing is not a threat to anyone's religious belief because the New Thought teaching can be incorporated into any religion without a person having to give up what their belief is.

A Conference Reverend Joanna and I attended in Arizona had three guest speakers, out of the eight that took part in the Conference, that were from different countries and different cultures but it all came together and supported the New Thought teaching.

It seems people are looking for spiritual food more than the controlling rules and regulations that most of us were brought up with. Our forefathers wanted to be sure a person's religious beliefs were protected and that one could believe in any way one chose that feeds one's spiritual hunger. I feel the New Thought Movement taking place in the world is a way for people to make their own choices as to what they want their life to be.

Most of the people are finding out that what they think about is what appears in their life. The book, <u>The Secret</u>, made it very clear that one could change the things in their life by just changing the way they were thinking about what they wanted and setting their intention accordingly.

People look at that concept and make a comment like, "I will believe it when I see it." I have heard that comment many times and I tell people to reverse the wording to, "you will see it when you believe it." It may not happen overnight because it is how much belief one has as to when they see it. When Peter asked Jesus why he could not walk on the water, Jesus asked him, "where is your belief." This is a good example as to why things don't come about as soon as one asks for it.

The way to a life of peace and joy is to have full trust in the Creative Energies of the Universe (God), set your intention and give it time to manifest. One will be surprised how life can change when there is trust and patience and always knowing that God is in charge.

And So It Is

Better Look Before You Leap

The Lord will perfect that which concerned me.
Psalm 138:8

I realize there are a lot of things going on in the world that have created a lot of concern for everyone. Not all people see it as negativity, but as an opportunity to improve their life and the life of others. It is times like we are experiencing now that bring forth new ideas and concepts that create a better way of life, not only for ourselves but for others as well.

The news media seems to dwell on the doom and gloom and that creates more negative thoughts which affect the lives of those who fall into that way of thinking. One cannot solve the problems of the world but one can solve the problems in the small world around them, that they have created for themselves. When one is looking for better ways of overcoming the problems in the small world around them, then the ideas start coming when one stays positive. The doom and gloom sells stories and newspapers and can keep one down if that is the kind of negative thoughts one dwells on.

I grew up with the mind set that you work hard and "when the going gets tough, the tough get going." That is not the way it works for me now because of the changes I have made in my life. Changing to a more positive way of thinking and not being spontaneous in taking action in a situation has created a life of joy and peace for me. Taking time to think about a situation is one of the keys that creates the joy and peace.

I remember the lyrics in a country western song that was popular several years back that said, "better look before you leap, still waters run deep." That is so true when a person is planning a career change or a new project for himself. It is always good to do the research and have a backup plan one can rely on if the first idea doesn't work. The still water may be deeper than expected and the plans have to be changed in order for the new undertaking to be successful.

When you "look before you leap" is the time to call on the Creative Force of the Universe, (God) for wisdom and guidance in the new venture. The scripture verse says it all when one needs a backup plan for any new venture. When one uses the guidance of the inner voice that is in all living things on this planet, then one is guided in the right direction for what has to be done. When one looks before one leaps one can create a different and more joyful life. The concerns one has are always taken care of when the faith and trust of God is called on. Life is a joy when one is balanced in mind, body and spirit. Let go and let God express through you the joy, love, peace and harmony.

And So It Is

Cultivate the Garden of the Mind

All that man achieves or fails to achieve is the direct result of his own thought. James Lane Allen

I see articles in magazines and the local papers about how spring starts a new beginning for a lot of projects. The most popular one is getting ready to plant one's vegetable garden. While living back east I always had a big garden each year and filled our freezers with different vegetables that were ready to harvest. During the late summer months the fresh vegetables were a treat with any meal.

It did take some preparation and work to keep the garden free of weeds and grass so the plants could get the water when it rained, or I used the hose if it didn't rain. Most of the time the rains were enough to keep the soil moist and the plants healthy. My neighbor always tried to be first in harvesting everything he planted. It made him feel real good when he could show me the ripe tomatoes, green beans, squash and other vegetables before mine were ready to pick.

The rewards I got from the garden were well worth the time and work that it took to bring about the harvest.

The same thing holds true with the thoughts one plants in mind and the effects they produce. I know there are those who plant seed thoughts in their minds and then don't nurture and support those thoughts to bring about the desired effects. When one plants a seed thought in the garden of the mind and they don't get results, it is because they did not believe it could happen for them. They were doing only wishful thinking when they planted the seed thoughts and did not follow through with what had to be done to get the results.

One might ask what should be done in order to get results. The main thing is to trust the Universe (God) and know without a doubt that all of one's good comes from the only power in the Universe and that is God. When one plants the seeds of thought in the Garden of the Mind, it has to be cultivated with good thoughts, prayer, meditation and affirmations that satisfy the soul. When the end results appear for you, give thanks for it and know it wasn't luck that brought it about.

There are those who see others prosper and call it luck or good fortune and have no idea that the thoughts one planted and nurtured brought about the prosperity. Our thoughts create our life whether it is good or not so good. The Universe acts on the thoughts one puts into mind and that creates the life one lives. The gifts of life are not by chance but are from efforts put forth or could be said to be "thoughts completed."

Life is a joy when one can realize one can have the life they want by just changing the way one thinks. One can achieve whatever there is when the Garden of the Mind is maintained with loving thoughts. The Buddha said "all that we are is the result of what we have thought. The mind is everything. What we think, we become." Have fun cultivating the Garden in your Mind and nurture it with love.

And So It Is

Enough Is Enough

*My help cometh from the Lord,
which made heaven and earth. Psalms 121:2*

While doing my spiritual time a couple of days ago, the thought of my neighbor in Ohio kept coming into my mind. I was trying to make a decision on how to handle a family situation and the thought kept coming as to how my neighbor Alice handled her situation. At the time I lived in Ohio I had never heard of the Science of Mind teaching and neither had Alice, but what she did worked for her.

Alice was the guardian of her younger sister Lisa, who was about twenty years her junior. Alice took on the role of guardian when Lisa was twelve years old. She was to make sure Lisa finished school and go to college if she desired. Living about twelve miles from the Akron University made it nice for Lisa because she could continue to live with Alice and still go to college. After college, Lisa had some problems keeping a job because of her attitude. It seemed like she thought the whole world was against her. She was always trying to defend herself in a way that made it difficult for her to have friends.

Alice had come to our house many times in tears because Lisa made her feel so bad because of the comments she would make about the way she was raised and that she was not loved. That was not the truth because Alice had a heart as big as the world for all people and expressed her love toward everyone.

Lisa knew what buttons to push to get Alice upset and did not let up when she saw that Alice was reacting to her comments. Finally Alice thought enough was enough and told Lisa she was tired of living a "hell on earth" and had decided that Lisa had to be on her own with her own place to live and get a job to support herself. That was not being cruel, it was using tough love to get Lisa to see herself for who and what she was. There was a time of no communication between them for a few months, but that was okay with Alice because she was able to be the wife to her husband that she always wanted to be

There are a lot of people living a life of "hell on earth" because of other people's anger, resentment, jealousy, insecurity and lack of wisdom as to who they really are. The Science of Mind teaching has made me become aware as to how good life can be when one understands how powerful the Creative Intelligence is that lives at the center of each being. This Intelligence guides the thoughts and actions to bring joy and peace into one's life.

About six months after Lisa moved out, she came to visit Alice and was an altogether different person. She and a girlfriend from college attended a workshop about how one hurts themselves when they don't allow the good feelings to be expressed. Lisa thanked Alice for being tough on her by telling her she had to be on her own because she was an adult and should act the part.

When we left Ohio in 1979 to come to California, Alice and Lisa were the best of friends and enjoyed each other because Lisa grew up and Alice was there with open arms as she always had been. The Creative Force of the Universe (God) works wonders when one is open to receive God's abundance of blessings.

And So It Is

It's All Good, It's All God Expressing

*And God saw everything He had made,
and behold, it was very good. Genesis 1:31*

There are so many things one passes by each day that could make a difference in one's life if the time was taken to notice. The flowers that bloom, the trees that bear fruit and nuts, the vines that add to the abundance we all share, all add to God's creation. This beautiful creation that surrounds us is the beauty of God expressing, not only through the plants but through all life on this planet.

I am not the greatest cook, but I do enjoy trying new recipes of different dishes that I find in magazines and newspapers. I was taught the basics of preparing a meal while growing up in a family of ten plus my mother and father. My mother would plan the meals and we children were expected to help with the preparation. I cannot put a value on what I learned in the short time I helped in the kitchen. All the cooking and baking was done on a wood burning stove because that was how it was done in the country where there were no utilities.

Teaching us children the basics of preparing a meal was my mother's way of teaching us how to survive. I enjoy cooking now because as I prepare the vegetables I notice how they are formed and how delicate they have to be in order to make them what they are. Taking a head of lettuce apart, one layer at a time, is a good example. The lettuce did not just happen to be that way: it was that way because the Divine Intelligence of the Universe (God) expressed itself through the lettuce as it was growing.

The same holds true with an orange when the peeling is removed and the segments are taken apart. One can see how delicate the orange is formed. Watching a flower unfold from a bud to an open blossom and looking into the center of the blossom, you can see how delicate the blossom is. That's the Creative Intelligence of the

Universe (God) expressing Itself through the beauty of the blossom.

I have been opening and removing the seed berries from some pomegranates I gathered from a bush I have in my backyard. This is the first time I have tried to freeze the berry seeds for later use. I was amazed at how they are formed and how the seed berries grow from the soft lining inside the beautiful cover. Only the Creative Intelligence of the Universe (God) could design and create something so delicate that can recreate itself over and over again from the seed inside.

All life on this planet is the unfolding of this Creative Intelligence that can be recognized in all animals (including man), all plants, all fowl, or the fish in the oceans because it is all God and is all Good. By recognizing all this beauty that surrounds each of us every day, you will experience joy, peace and harmony in this thing called Life.

And So It Is

Know You Are The Temple of God

Do you not know you are the Temple of God, and that the spirit of God dwells in you. I Corinthians 3:16

Throughout the scriptures we read about the temples that people built for a place to worship. We read of great temples in all parts of the world and about people traveling from all points to visit and admire the architectural designs that helps make these temples more sacred.

Any place of worship could be considered a temple regardless of the size and design. The temples of the world are places where people feel they are closer to the Creative Force of the Universe (God) and come away uplifted in their spiritual awareness. That is the mind set of all cultures and all who participate are getting the spiritual food that serves their needs and helps keep them in the peace of mind that creates joy and love in their life.

The temples of the world are built of various kinds of stone and other materials that have withstood the elements for thousands of years and should stand for many more years to come. It is interesting to see documentaries on television about some of these old temples and what they were used for by different cultures. The one temple that doesn't get much attention is the temple where the spirit of God lives.

The word temple or temples is mentioned 92 times in the Old and New Testament and to my knowledge the one that didn't relate to a structure is in the scripture at the beginning of this article. The physical body and mind hold all the attributes of God and that makes our body the holy temple of the almighty spirit that I understand and know as a very loving and giving God.

It is the spirit within that guides and directs all life on this planet, so I feel that the body of man is not the only temple of God. Each animal of the land, fishes of the waters, and birds of the air, all have the built in guidance and intelligence of how to survive because it is the spirit of God within them expressing at all times. They are all directed as to when and what to do just as man is when man gets himself out of the way and allows the Creative Intelligence of the Universe (God) to guide his thoughts and the action he or she takes.

It is always for one's best and highest good when one listens to that small still voice within, and follows the feeling or thoughts one gets as to what to do. The temple you are for the Holy Spirit is the temple of all temples because it is the only temple that houses the Creative Intelligence of the Universe (God). When one takes care of that temple and keeps it well maintained, then you are the beloved in whom the Creator is well-pleased. Only you can do it for you.

And So It Is

Listen To The Inner Voice

Be not faithless, but believing.
John 20:27

It is so wonderful to know that I am in control of everything that happens in my life experience. I know to a lot of people that may sound like I am on a trip in la la land. Twenty some years ago I would have said the same thing. I have become aware that I create all experiences in my life by the way I think and the action I take on those thoughts.

The people of the world would not have the modern equipment and the technology to use the equipment if people had not followed up on the ideas or thoughts they received. When a person receives a thought and does not take action on the thought, then it continues on until someone else takes action.

We would not have the time saving equipment and other technology if no one had taken action on an idea. Once he or she takes action, then the ways and means come to them through other thoughts and ideas. That is the creative process that has always been and always will be, because that is the Creative Force of the Universe (God) in action. Every being has the ability to create anything they desire by focusing his or her mind on what they want to experience in their life.

There was a time I would not have believed this could happen until I proved it to myself several times. Every being is equipped with an inner feeling that can guide one's action on an idea or thought when he or she takes time to listen or feel what one should do.

I read a story about Kevin Costner and the movie <u>Field of Dreams</u>. All of Kevin's peers said it would ruin his career if he did the movie the way the script was written. His peers said the script did not have any of what people wanted such as swearing, fighting, or bedding down with a starlet. The film's producer, Phil Robinson, was undecided until Kevin said the only way he would do the film was to leave the script the way it was originally written. Kevin had the inner feeling that people were ready for a film like this and he stood up because he believed in his inner feeling.

I don't have to tell you the outcome of the film because every adult in this country and abroad has seen it at least once. One does not have to copy anyone else or change anything because someone else "thinks" it should be done their way.

When one gets a thought or idea and wants to take action, then the "gut feeling" will guide one in what direction they need to go.

As the scripture verse says to "believe in your faith," and it shall be done unto you as you believe. The Spirit that dwells within will never take one in the wrong direction when one listens to the small still voice within and follows his or her heart. It is always for your best and highest good because it is God in action.

And So It Is

Love Makes Our Little World Go Around

*What shall it profit a man, if he shall gain the whole world,
and lose his own soul? Mark 8:36*

There are so many ways one can look at the question above that Jesus asked the people and his disciples at one of his gatherings. When one thinks about what Jesus was asking it is so true with so many people in today's experience.

Through the thoughts we get from the Universe and the action we take on those thoughts, we create our own little world. Each person has their own life to live and we each create things that make our life what it should be, a joy and not a burden on ourselves or others.

The work we do each day should be in balance so the body and mind can function as one and create joy. I know to some that sounds like I am coming from way out in left field. We each have an inner soul that needs to be nourished as well as the physical body we have that houses the inner soul. Jesus called the inner soul "the Father within" and one of our spiritual mentors, Ralph Waldo Emerson, called it the "Oversoul." Whatever one might think it is, it has to be part of the life we live on this plane.

I know when love is left out of the equation, the balance of life is tilted to a point that we get ourselves in a very confusing situation. Every being has a temper that is part of the defense mechanism built in each of us for survival.

Some people realize that when one is able to control the feelings that cause the temper to rise, uncomfortable situations can be eliminated. The built in feeling of love and compassion within each being is to offset the temper and anger so life can be a joy and the soul is being fed what it needs to stay strong.

One of the keys to a joyful life is to create a life that is balanced in mind, body and spirit. There are some people who concentrate on material things for themselves and pay no attention to the inner feeling of satisfaction. There are those who stay angry and express their temper toward others that don't agree with them and cause a situation that they wish they could retract.

The feeling of wanting to retract is the built in feeling of compassion trying to overcome the temper and angry feeling that was expressed. When one is good to themselves, then it is easy to express that good to others.

One way to be good to yourself is to reward yourself when you reach a goal that you set. A small gift for yourself satisfies the inner feeling, which is food for the soul. It may a bouquet of flowers or it may be a single rose but the main thing is to reward yourself in a way that brings joy and harmony to your life.

Don't waste away your life trying to get, get, get, because if you don't give, give, give, then you are out of balance with mind, body and spirit and the soul is being left out of the experience. The love and compassion one has for themselves and others is the number one key to being able to control the feeling that caused the temper to rise that gets one out of balance with life. Create good things in your own little world by allowing the Father within to guide and direct the every day activities that make life a joy to live.

And So It Is

THE GREATEST GIFT IS TO HELP OTHERS

Doing good to others is not a duty. It is a joy, for it increases your own health and happiness. Zoroaster

I read stories in books written by people who have lived the experience and the stories come from the heart and are not make believe. The experience one has is something that lives forever in one's mind and can never be taken away. Those who share those experiences are usually the type of people who are eager to help others in time of need.

I realize the act of giving has a greater impact on the soul than trying to get something for one's self. It is great to have the things one needs but it is even greater to share with others the things that bring happiness to one's self. The stories in some of the books I read bring out the true feeling of giving and one can feel that energy while reading. One of the stories I read was written by a person who lost both hands in an accident.

While in the hospital and realizing both hands were gone was reason enough to think that life was over for him. His thoughts were, how could he continue life without hands and have to depend on hooks. He was ready to give up, when he had a visit from a person who lost both hands during World War II. The visit turned his life around after he saw what he could do that didn't require the physical use of his hands.

He always liked to read stories to his nephews and nieces before the accident and thought that would be a good thing for the children in hospitals and orphanages. He would get the children in a group and appoint one of them to turn the pages for him. They liked helping him so much by turning the pages, that he had to have a little   contest each day among the children to see who would get the job that day. It not only taught the children to be fair with each other, but also taught them how great it was to give help to someone else. It was good therapy for the author but the main lesson was what he was teaching the children about giving.

I know there are people sitting home each day feeling sorry for themselves because of something they feel ruined their life. Life on this planet is a joy when one can help others in need. It not only brings joy and happiness to one's life but also feeds the soul the spiritual food it needs for one to be balanced in mind, body and spirit. When one's life is in balance with the Creative Force of the Universe (God) then life takes on a new level of experience.

As one gives of their time, talent and treasure then it is returned packed down, heaped up and running over. The abundance of the universe continues to pour into one's life at a rate that is beyond imagination. It all starts with sharing with others and grows to a point that the sharing is a big part of the joy life is on this planet.

I know the author of the story was so thankful for the visit he received that turned his life around and he is now helping children anywhere he goes. Create health and happiness in your life by giving to others the love and affection you want to receive yourself. It doesn't take much effort, only a willingness to share.

And So It Is

We Have Been Given A Great Gift

In quietness and confidence shall be my strength.
Isaiah 30:15

I was putting new nectar in my hummingbird feeder when I was surprised that one of the little creatures landed on it while I still had it in my hands. The little bird had no fear of me whatsoever. After I hung the feeder up I watched those little birds doing their acrobatic movements and enjoying the fresh nectar I had put in the feeder.

This brought thoughts to my mind about just how free and fearless these birds live their life. They live their life the way the Creative Force of the Universe (God) intended for all life on this planet to live. Like the lilies of the field they toil not, they spin not because that is their created nature.

Man is no different than the hummingbird or the lilies, except man has the ability to think. This ability to think can create bondage and fear for himself by the thoughts he dwells on.

The fear that is building up in the world today about the financial crisis is all man made and could be turned around by changing the negative energy that is being put into it. Negative thoughts create more negativity and the fear continues to build. Most of the projections are the opinions of some negative people who express themselves on television with the intent to create fear and doubt in the minds of the viewer. It is the doom and gloom comments that feed the fear around the world.

It is not the truth of man to live in fear because of his connected relationship with all of Nature. Everything in Nature is the creation of God and God does not create fear because God is all love and there is no space for fear to occupy.

When one fully trusts the Creative Intelligence of the Universe (God) and knows within himself that all there is is God then fear disappears in the light of that revelation. Joel Goldsmith writes, "we must dwell in the secret place of the Most High not just on Sunday, but every day at morning, noon and night."

The great gift that has been given to each of us is that we can overcome fear by just changing the way we think and how we analyze or respond to a situation. Allow the small still voice within to give the answers and guidance needed to get above the fear. Jesus referred to the place of Most High as the closet of your mind where it is quiet and one can make that connection with this Creative Force that I know as God, in order to get answers and peace of mind.

The love of God will cast out the fear that can be a block that holds one back from his or her good. The indwelling presence of God in each being on this planet is a power that can be used to create love, joy, peace and harmony, which overrides fear.

One gets the answers when they allow the love of God to come forward; get quiet and listen because that is one's strength. Love God with all of your heart and soul and get above the fear that is holding back the good you deserve.

And So It Is

Perseverance Creates A Life of Joy

Stand fast, and hold the traditions which ye have been taught.
II Thessalonians 2:15

There have been so many situations where the end results would not have been a success if the people doing the project had listened to others and taken a different approach. Chances are we may not have had the type of light bulb that has served us all these years, if Edison had wavered from his idea and let other people's comments stop him.

Regardless what a person is working on, there is always someone who feels they should do it a different way and they don't hesitate to express their idea on how it should be done. I don't think one could call that human nature because it is not the nature of God to interrupt one's right thinking. The right thinking I am referring to is for the good of the person doing the project and the good it is going to bring to everyone involved.

I was taught to keep my mouth shut and not make any comments unless asked by the person doing a project if I had any thoughts as to how to solve a problem he had run into. There are people who visualize the end results of an idea and don't need to be interrupted by someone with an over inflated ego who wants recognition. The end result cannot happen if one allows others to distract him or her with their comments and ideas.

I read a story about Mel Fisher who spent fourteen years searching for a sunken treasure ship off the Florida Keys and finally found it. It was the perseverance that kept him and the crew going each week because they knew in their heart that "today is the day" and they would all be very rich.

There are times when a person gets an idea and tries to make it a reality but it doesn't turn out that way, so they move on to something else. For something good to work in one's life, it takes perseverance and commitment to enjoy the end results. The intention one sets in mind and the discipline one sets on themselves is only part of what it takes for the end results to be a success.

There are so many opportunities for each person when they open their mind and allow the ideas to come to them. All constructive ideas come from one source; the Divine Mind of the Universe (God). These ideas and the action taken can only produce good experiences because the idea was from the Divine Mind which can only produce good. With some ideas it takes perserverance to get the end results. The rewards one gets from the end results are part of the abundance all beings are entitled to. The abundance of the Universe is poured out to everyone that is open to receive.

When one seeks the Kingdom then all else comes with ease because the recognition of the indwelling presence of Spirit is the Kingdom. It is not a one-time experience. It takes commitment and perseverance each day to stay in balance with mind, body and spirit. The rewards are always worth the effort put into it because it adds peace, joy and harmony to the life of the one who perseveres.

And So It Is

Understanding the Keys To The Kingdom

For one that asks, receives; and he that seeks finds; and to him that knocks it shall be opened. Luke 11:10

I met Reverend David Owen Ritz at a conference at Lake Arrowhead and had the pleasure of spending a couple of hours with him in front of a crackling fire in the lobby of the conference headquarters. David was the founding minister of the Sarasota, Florida Church of Religious Science, that had a membership of over three thousand.

He formed the church, from an idea in a very short period of time because of his high level of consciousness attracted people to him. In the spiritual world, like minded people are attracted to like minded people by way of Divine Intelligence that makes the ways possible for people to be at the right place at the right time. As the scripture verse says "he that seeks, finds."

David was the kind of person who only wanted to serve others and when one serves others, that is a way of serving God. David had worked on and put together a twelve week workshop called Keys To The Kingdom and the workshop was an eye-opener to those who had no idea how they were blocking their good by the way they were thinking and acting.

I facilitated the workshop at the Spiritual Awareness Center in 2001 and it was a success for the 16 people who enrolled and finished the 12-week course. They learned that the resentment they carried toward others was a big block that was holding them back from the things they wanted to accomplish.

When there is resentment toward others, the only way one can overcome that kind of thinking is to do forgiveness work for themselves and forgive the person who they thought did them wrong. That was one of the "keys to the kingdom" that most of the students could relate to and recognize that that is a part of God. Resentments had to be released in order for them to move forward on their spiritual growth.

The students learned the negative power of anger, jealousy, mistrust, lying to ones self and others, manipulating others for financial advancement for one's self, taking advantage of others who could not help themselves at the time, not being loyal to family members, and a host of other negative acts that could keep the abundance of the Universe from flowing freely into one's life. "Seek first the Kingdom and all else comes with ease," is so true once one has found the kingdom.

To recognize the spirit that dwells at the center of our being is part of seeking the Kingdom. To be honest with one's self and others is another key. To serve others without expecting anything in return is another key. To love others unconditionally while loving one's self is another key.

Another key is to see the good in every situation and know the Creative Force of the Universe (God) is always in charge and is always supporting and directing everything for the best and highest good of everyone in the experience.

To forgive yourself and others is very important because through forgiveness you surrender, let go and let the Creative Force of the Universe (God) take charge of your life. When you forgive you start enjoying the good that is behind the next door you knock on as it opens to more joy, peace and harmony.

And So It Is

THE THANKS YOU GIVE IS THE THANKS YOU GET, MULTIPLIED

Give, and it shall be given unto you; pressed down, and running over. Luke 6:38

The month of November is the month most people feel is the month of giving thanks. It has been the tradition since the Pilgrims and Native Americans shared the bounty from their efforts together with a feast. They were giving thanks for the abundant yield from the crops they worked on together. It is great to recognize what we have today in our life and the progress this country has made since the great feast by the Pilgrims and Native Americans.

I know there are those who are unable to share their abundance with others because of hardships from disasters and other acts of nature that they had no control over. That is why it is so important for those who have, to help those who have not. It doesn't have to be a disaster of some kind for people to help others that are in need. Serving and helping others is the best way to satisfy the inner feeling that creates joy and harmony in one's life. It doesn't only have to be in the month of November when we are thankful for what we have, it can be at all times during the year.

People get hungry every day and need the help of others in order to live to see the days yet to come. There are a lot of charities, not only local, but nationwide that make it their purpose to see that people are taken care of. It takes time and work to keep those kind of charities supported, to be able to help those in need.

I have a favorite charity I contribute to quite often because they are always there for those that need a helping hand to overcome the hardship they are experiencing. The money is put to a good purpose in all areas of its operation and is not spent on high salaried executives.

I have always supported any charity that depends upon volunteers to keep the organization functioning. The people who volunteer are the people who want to serve and help others because they get their reward by giving of themselves and that satisfies the inner feeling that I know as the soul.

Every being is created with the same amount of spirit within and it is how one chooses to recognize the spirit within that determines the kind of life they wish to live. The more one recognizes the spirit within, the more one is willing to help and serve others because it satisfies the need they feel that brings about their joy and happiness.

I know as we give we receive and that those who recognize this are those who live a life of joy and happiness and know within themselves that their needs are always met. The abundance of the Universe continues to flow into their life because they are willing to share with others and that keeps the abundance flowing.

When one stops the abundance from flowing, by not giving and by keeping it all for themselves, it creates a non-flowing situation and everything in one's life becomes stagnated. One can get back into the flow of abundance by feeling good about themselves and being willing to share their time, talent and treasure with those that are unfortunate.

The Creative Force of the Universe (God) is the source of all our good and the more one recognizes this, the more one is willing to be of service to others, because when one serves others one is serving God. When one can give, not expecting anything in return, then the meaning of giving thanks is more satisfying to the soul because it is the spiritual food the soul needs in order to create a life of peace, joy and happiness for the one that shares the abundance.

And So It Is

Tis The Season To Be Positive

A merry heart doesth good like medicine.
Proverbs 17:22

It is that time of year that the joy of life should be expressed in everything one does. The joy should be expressed every day of one's life because that is the life all beings were created to live. This time of the year is a challenge to some people because they live their life thinking about the past and how they could have had a better life if they had done this or that and not taken the path they are on now.

The past is the past and there is nothing anyone can do to change what happened then. We have learned that past experiences are what creates the life we live today. The joy of life is to live in the now moment and let go of the past because it has already served its purpose and we don't have to go back and relive it. A cheerful person is one who enjoys the now moments and passes that cheer on to others in their every day activities.

A cheerful person may not be a happy person at all times because things happen that take away the happiness. The positive person can overcome this feeling by staying cheerful and extending feelings of love toward others. There are those who are not happy or cheerful with anything that happens in their life. Those kind of people make it difficult for those who try to extend good feelings toward others because they try to drag others down to their level of negative thinking.

I stopped at the store on my way home, and at the check-out counter there was a person really giving the clerk a hard time over a sale item. He had picked up what he thought was the sale item but it was a different brand than what was on sale. The clerk wanted to exchange the item for the sale item. The customer couldn't understand why he couldn't check out what he had as a sale item. He finally walked out without buying anything and the clerk had to recheck the other item she left in order for her register to balance at the end of her shift. It not only took the clerk's time, but it held up the line at the checkout because he had made the mistake and would not allow it to be corrected by the clerk.

This was a man who was not happy with himself and seemed to want everyone in his experience to be as unhappy as he was. It is difficult for me to understand how those kind of people can live with themselves being that way and not thinking about who they hurt.

When a person is living their life in balance with mind, body and spirit, negative people have no effect on them because they recognize the God Presence within that person and have no concern of what they are doing. The Creative Force of the Universe (God) has created each being with the ability to express love out to everyone and those that do are the ones with the merry heart and see things through the eyes of love and compassion toward everyone. The compassion one has for others is the act of a merry heart and that creates the love, peace and harmony we were created to enjoy.

And So It Is

We Have Been Given The Greatest Gift of All

For God hath not given us the spirit of fear, but of power and of love, and of a sound mind. II Timothy 1:7.

The season of giving gifts is at the forefront of so many peoples minds, so it is only proper to join in the joy of the season and give. The gifts we give are received with gratitude at the time and then we get back into the everyday routine and it is a grind for some people until this time next year.

The worry and struggle some people go through are what they expect life to be and continue to live in that kind of consciousness because they have never been taught that there are other ways to live life. That kind of life is built on the fear that there isn't enough and they have to keep working and struggling in order to survive.

People have to work, but it doesn't have to be a struggle if a person is doing what he or she loves to do, then it is not work, but a pleasure. When one is doing what one loves to do then he or she is in the flow of life and it is a joy to do what one is doing. When one is doing what one loves to do then the rewards follow. There is always enough money to do what one needs to do with some left over to share with others.

We have been given the greatest gift of all from the Creative Force of the Universe (God) which is the spirit of power, love, and a sound mind. The power is the knowing of who and what we are and allowing God to work through us; it is a power that never fails and gives us strength and support in whatever we are doing. The scripture says in Isaiah 30:15 "in quietness and confidence shall be my strength."

When one gets quiet and listens to the small still voice within, then the answers come through. That is the power within that Jesus talked about when he said "it is not I but the Father within who does the work." A person who relies on the power within himself does not have to worry and struggle in order to survive.

The wonderful gift we have been given in a sound mind is the ability to think, use our common sense and allow the wisdom within to guide the intelligence we were all created with. This will lead one to receiving more creative ideas and those ideas can lead to more abundance pouring into one's life bringing more plea sure and joy.

The greatest gift we have been given is the gift of love. Recognizing the gift of love allows us to transcend our differences and recognize the Christ consciousness in every being. When we love ourselves and our neighbor, then we are allowing God to express through us and we are being true to the highest and best that is in us.

When we recognize and trust the faith of God that is within us, then we can have full confidence that God will supply everything we need. The love within each of us can override any fear that is in our consciousness and that love will increase more as one continues to rely on "the Father within" to guide and direct the everyday activities that bring joy, peace, and harmony to the flow of a loving life.

And So It Is

Accept Change With Joy and Understanding

The greatest blessing of the Spirit pours through me now and protects me in all my ways. Ernest Holmes, <u>Science of Mind</u>, pg. 257

I was looking at the back yard through the window in my kitchen, while it was raining, and noticed that the leaves falling from the huge trees in my backyard were nonstop. The rain was knocking the leaves off the trees faster than they normally fall.

As I watched this happening, I was thinking about how great the Creative Force of the Universe (God) is when it is time for the trees to shed their leaves and prepare for a rest period before the next cycle. The same holds true with the fruit and nut trees I see when driving on the back roads through the orchards when going up to the lake or just taking Tyson, my wonderful dog, for a ride.

Every living thing on this planet has a cycle that is activated at the right time by the Divine Intelligence that is within that living thing so it can reproduce and survive. All the plants, trees and animals, including man, have this intelligence within that lets the living thing know when it is time to start and end the cycle. The beauty of the flowers we enjoy is one of the acts of this Creative Intelligence that reflects the beauty of God and the joy that flowers bring to so many that take the time to pay attention.

Man has learned from working with the plants and animals as to how these cycles are timed and what needs to be done in order to get the most production at the end of the cycle. For example, in order to get the beauty of some flowers one has to plant the bulbs in the fall and the Intelligence within that bulb knows when it is time to sprout and bring a beautiful flower in the spring. That is just one of the thousands of things man has learned over the years and it does not pertain to just plants but also animals.

Man has the ability to think and make decisions on how

and what needs to be done in order for the different species to survive and this has made man the steward of the planet. Man does not control Nature but provides the ways and means to protect the different species so they are free to be what they were created to be.

I know there is some abuse in areas where the intelligence of man has not caught up with what is right and what needs to be done to protect other life on this planet. We see and hear about a lot of improvement being made in the areas of abuse and it is becoming more and more heartwarming when people take part in the projects and help with the animals and plants that cannot help themselves.

The hay drop in Yellowstone Park last year is a good example because it allowed the bison to survive the winter due to the deep snow that covered their natural food. The different acts of kindness that are coming forth are making a difference in the way man is starting to think and it sure is making a better world for every living thing on this planet.

The kind acts one does in helping others and the animals gives a feeling inside that is difficult to describe. Put some food out for the birds and get that feeling inside that brings joy to one's life.

And So It Is

Recognize Yourself By Using The Power Within

The only guarantee of our Divinity is in its expression through our humanity. Ernest Holmes, <u>Science of Mind</u>, pg. 238

It is only a few days away and this year will be history. There is no way we can get that time back or relive the experiences we had during the past year. With the new year ready to begin, some people are thinking about some of the changes they should make in their life to bring a more productive experience in the coming year. This is what some people call a New Year's resolution.

I have made those resolutions in the past only to see them fade away because I didn't think they were important enough to follow through on. There were other activities at the time that had priority over my time and efforts. As I think back over some of the experiences that I thought were more important than the resolutions I made, I would get myself mixed up in my thinking and that caused confusion in my life. There was something going on in my life at the time that I wanted to change, or I would not have made the resolution.

When one takes action to correct a problem or a situation and follows through with right action, the end results make one's life more of a joy. This is evidence of a person living a balanced life. To live a well balanced life, one has to apply one's efforts to the four basic aspects which are work, play, worship and love. The work one is doing should be something that he or she loves to do, then it is not considered work but pleasure.

Being able to work in harmony with others is a way to feel you fit in with the group. Having a good feeling about others can make the work a joy. When the work day is over one should have something they enjoy doing in order to relax and have some fun. It may be by one's self or with the family, but there should be time set aside to play. Too much work and no play makes a person undesirable to have as company or as a partner.

The worship part of a person's life is very important as to how well one is balanced. To be true to one's self, there has to be the recognition that the Creative Intelligence of the Universe (God) is the source of all one's good.

There is only one God that all religions recognize and that God should be part of one's daily prayers. Give thanks to God for the abundance that flows into and through one's daily activities. When one puts God first in everything that is happening, then the joy and peace of life unfolds. Being one with God brings about the last aspect of a balanced life and that is love. When one can express unconditional love toward everything on this planet, then the balance of life is much easier to maintain.

When one is living a balanced life in all areas, then the forgiveness of one's self and others comes about easily because there is no anger, resentment, jealousy or judgment in one's thoughts. When one can let go and let God guide one's everyday activities, then one doesn't have to make resolutions in order to make changes in one's life.

The thoughts one has are what creates one's life. The positive thoughts bring into reality a positive life, so change your thinking and change your life. You have the power within to create a wonderful life for yourself.

And So It Is

Give Thanks To God For New Beginnings

*The new birth comes not by observation or by loud
proclamation, but through an inner sense of reality.*
Ernest Holmes, *Science of Mind*, pg. 472

Now that the New Year has dawned and the celebrations are over, it is time to think about the new beginnings that some people set for themselves. I look forward to this time of year because it gives way to a lot of changes that take place, not only in nature but in opportunities to change things in one's own life.

The energy one spends on things that have no future or a way to better one's life are a waste of time and effort. Starting something new is always exciting and gives one a feeling of a new venture that could replace some of the old ways of doing things.

There are times when one gets stuck in a rut and one loses the ambition to do things that could change their lives or the lives of others. When that happens, it is time to think about what one is doing and how one could change some of the things that are bringing in negative energy that is causing the feeling of failure.

There is a power in the universe, greater than we are, that is always willing to help when asked to. That power is the answer to all that is going on in one's life and is the power I recognize as a loving and giving God. It is the Creative Intelligence of the Universe and is always around us and dwells in the center of our being.

There is no way we could be separated from this Creative Intelligence because it is part of each being. Jesus said "it is not I but the Father within that does the work," and all one has to do is recognize that presence within and use it to help overcome any problem or fear that causes one to be in a rut.

I know how good it feels to let go of a situation and turn in over to this Creative Intelligence (God) and then watch the situation change for my highest and best good. It never fails and the Power we have within can be used for others as well as ourselves. That is why our Center has been a part of the World Peace Prayer and Meditation for the past 15 years because the more people that participate the more powerful the prayer is.

I would like to see more people in this country take part in the World Peace Prayer each year because it can change the things in our world. Our community is the world around us that can be more peaceful when more people recognize that affirmative prayer is the answer and can bring about peace, harmony, and prosperity.

Some day soon man will wake up to the fact that negative energy used for war and destruction can be turned around to a positive energy used to benefit all peoples of the world and there would be no hunger or suffering. It takes the power of prayer to wake up the spiritual magnificence in each being, including the leaders of all nations, and then the thoughts of peace are certain to happen.

Our daily spiritual practices should include thoughts of peace for our community and the world and that would raise the collective consciousness of our planet to where there would be no room for thoughts of destruction. I urge everyone to stand up and be counted as part of the everyday world peace prayer that will bring about the action of God to make way for peace, harmony and prosperity for every being on this planet.

And So It Is

We Are One With All Living Things

Of Him, and through Him, and to Him, are all things.
Romans 11:36

I know that animals have been part of man's life from the beginning of time. Not only for food but they can be trained to do some of the work that makes man's life more of a joy. The camel was probably the first to be used as transportation and on down through the animal kingdom more and more animals were trained to be of service to man.

The horse was probably the most used in all countries as man evolved in his quest for a better way of life. The dolphin has been a big help for man in being able to detect mines and other obstacles in the oceans around the world placed there by the so called enemies of our country.

Since all life on this planet is connected to one Source (God) then it doesn't make any sense to fight any war, but there have been wars by man from the beginning of time. It is sad that man has to involve the innocent animals in his greed for more power over his fellow man. Enough said about what is wrong; lets look at what love can do when animals are involved.

Dogs, cats and horses are probably the most popular of domestic animals that are recognized as part of man's life. I do know that the presence of an animal around a group of people can change the attitude and feeling of the group.

Last week Rev. Joanna and I attended our yearly conference in Scottsdale, Arizona and it was a very uplifting and spiritual experience for both of us. Not only was the positive energy at a high level, there was also the presence of a guide dog that added to the experience. Rev. Jim Thompson is a minister of a church in Sacramento, California and has been attending the conferences for the past six years. He is blind and has a wonderful dog whom is his eyes and helps him keep out of trouble. I have heard and read that a person should not feed or pet a guide dog because it distracts the dog from doing its job.

I had the privilege of spending a couple of hours with Rev. Jim and the dog Eddie one afternoon on a bench under a beautiful shade tree on the conference grounds. He told me his eyes were in the end of a cane for fifteen years and then he took the training and got Eddie. He told me it was a life changing experience; Eddie kept him from danger and he had a companion that was always there for him.

I asked him if it bothered Eddie when people would pet and talk to him. He said he encouraged people to pet Eddie because it not only made Eddie feel good but the people got a good feeling of Eddie's loving energy and it made them feel good. The dog exhibited a spiritually high energy each day at the conference and a lot of people came away from the conference with a heart full of love for Rev. Jim and Eddie.

While watching Eddie work, I could feel the God connecting energy between Rev. Jim and Eddie. This is the connection we have with all life on this planet when one opens up and allows that connection to come forward. The Bible verse in Romans tells of that connection and when one believes it then one feels and sees it.

All animals have a way to communicate between themselves. Man is starting to figure out some of the communications which are bringing man closer and closer to the understanding that, yes we are one with all life on this planet. Take care of the animals because they are a part of you. The joy of life is to recognize the oneness we are with everything on this planet.

And So It Is

THE PERFECTION IS DEMONSTRATED

*And God created great whales and every
living creature that moves. Genesis 1:21*

The Animal Planet on television is one of the few channels I watch and it is so interesting because it shows nature (God) in action. There is so much one can learn by just watching the action of animals on land as well as in the sea. The program several nights ago was about sea animals. It started out with a whale and ended up with the kind of life there is at 3,000 plus feet.

The part about the whale was most interesting to me because it demonstrated the perfection that God created. The whale could be on the surface taking in air and then could dive to a depth of 3,000 feet without the pressure at that depth crushing it. I know it took man a long time to be able to go to a depth of 3,000 plus feet because of the pressure that would crush anything that was not designed to withstand it. Yet the whale with the perfec-tion of God in action could do it as an everyday activity to get food.

I remember when a new submarine was built that was supposed to be the biggest and the most modern with more ca-pabilities than any submarine in the world. They named it the Thrasher, after the Thrasher Shark because of what it was capable of doing. One of the features was that it could dive deeper than any sub known to the world and stay down for longer periods of time.

I had a distant relative, who was one of the designing engi-neers, and he told us what the sub was capable of doing. The day it was launched from the port where it was built was the last time anyone saw it. There were 19 engineers and techni-cians on board plus the crew. The investigation showed that the sub broke apart from the pressure of the depth they had dived to.

I don't think man will ever be able to design and build anything to compare with what God created from the beginning of time. The sharks and whales don't break apart when they dive to the great depths to get food and return to the surface to get more air in order to dive again. To me that is the perfection of God in action and cannot be duplicated by man even though man is becoming smarter as he continues to evolve.

The advanced intelligence that man is moving toward is also God in action expressing through man. When the thoughts and the actions taken are all summed up, it all relates to the Creative Intelligence of the Universe (God) in action. The source of everything that takes place on this planet is God in action because God is all there is.

And So It Is

CREATIVE ENERGY IS ALWAYS THERE READY TO ACT

The sovereign (superior) cure for worry is prayer.
William James

I read a story about Abraham Lincoln the day he left Springfield, Illinois on February 11, 1861 and how he stood on the platform of the railroad car and asked the people, who had gathered for the farewell departure, to pray for him to make the right decisions. Here was a man of faith that knew that deep within himself were the answers to the questions that were being asked about the divided country and how he was going to bring it together to make it whole once again.

He seemed to realize that he would never return to Springfield again and the farewell address was his final address to the people who trusted him and had faith in what he stood for. When asking for their prayers he realized the power in group prayer and said "without divine assistance I cannot succeed; with it I cannot fail."

We realize there are many great people of the past and in the present time and those that will follow in the future who know now and will know then the power of the Creative Intelligence in the Universe and rely on that Intelligence for the guidance needed to solve the misunderstandings of the world. The people and cultures of the world would not put their people's lives in jeopardy if they would understand that the power of prayer can solve all misunderstandings.

The power of prayer has no limit and can bring about answers and healings like the miracles Jesus performed during his ministry. To Jesus, it was the way life was supposed to be lived. It is still in today's experiences that we hear of something happening that could only come from divine intervention into the situation that brought the end results for the good of everyone. An example would be the story of the rescue of WWI fighter ace Eddie Rickenbacker and his crew that were forced to ditch their plane in the ocean and survive for over two weeks in the ocean with no food and water.

One of the men had a Bible and they formed a Bible study two times a day and learned to pray together. They had two fishing lines and hooks but no bait. During their prayer time a gull landed on Eddie's head and that gave them something to eat plus bait for their fishing lines. The fish they caught and the water they collected from the storms at sea kept them alive until they were rescued. They were hundreds of miles from any land but yet a gull appeared from nowhere and was the key factor in their survival.

God works in mysterious ways but when there is prayer, faith, and trust, it is not a mystery as to what can happen when one prays knowing that it is done unto him as he believes. Pray knowing it is yours when you pray and it appears in your experience when the time is right (in divine time) and the trust and faith you have is what you truly believe for yourself and all others in the experience.

There is no reason for worry when you have full trust and belief that it is done unto you as you truly believe. The story of Eddie Rickenbacker is a good example of how this Creative Energy (God) is always there ready to help.

And So It Is

The Presence of God In All Creation

God is an immediate presence and an immediate experience in my mind and soul, and I am conscious of this Perfect Presence, this Divine Wisdom, and Eternal Wholeness.
Ernest Holmes, <u>Science of Mind</u>, pg. 559

The past sixty or so days have been a total delight for me because I have been watching a family of red tailed hawks nesting in the tall trees in the back of my lot. I watched the parents build the nest, sit on the eggs, watched them feed the chicks and then watched the chicks leave the nest in flight. It seems like a simple way for the hawks to add to the population of their kind but the truth is there were times of disharmony. The hawks moved into the territory of crows that had lived in the trees for the past five years. The crows gave up the trees to the hawks but not without a lot of protest but the hawks won and the crows moved to the trees about a half a block away.

It was a joy for me to watch the family of hawks, after the chicks hatched, from my patio during my morning coffee time. There wasn't too much going on when the parents took turns sitting on the eggs except for the shift change. One would sit on the nest while the other searched for food and would bring the food back to share with the one on duty at the time.

It is amazing how the Creative Force of the Universe (God) expresses Itself through the activities of life on this planet. However, a lot of it goes unnoticed by those who should be paying attention to the way Nature unfolds and make that a part of their daily activity.

It was exciting for me when the young chicks were exercising their wings and building their strength to make that first flight. I watched them leave the nest to climb out on the limbs several feet from the nest. By watching through binoculars I could see the energy inside their bodies urging them to make that first flight. There was no way the chick could resist what was driving them to make that first flight.

The same way with the fruit on the trees. The tree cannot stop the fruit from forming because that is the built in Intelligence in the tree and the fruit to be what they were intended to be. The same goes for all animals and plant life on this planet.

Somewhere along the way, man got side tracked for some reason and has failed to allow the Creative Intelligence to express through him, as him and be what he was created to be. Each being has a part to play in the orchestra of life and some have gotten out of tune with the rest of the musicians of harmony. They get in a band of their own with no direction or reason for what life is about for them. By watching the way Nature unfolds, one can get centered in the flow of life and march to the beat of his own drum and do what his desire is as long as one is balanced in mind, body and spirit.

The crows and hawks know what to do because the instinct within guides them through all experiences, so why not allow this all-knowing, always creating energy of the universe to guide and direct the activities of man's life and get in the flow and stay in the flow to have a wonderful life.

And So It Is

Willingness To Be Willing

It is the greatest of all mistakes to do nothing because you can only do a little. Do what you can. Sydney Smith

Spring graduation for the colleges across this great nation is about to take place. One may wonder what all of those young people are going to do if they can't find employment in the field they chose for a career. Some may have prospects for jobs and will be ready to move forward with their dreams. For others it may not be that simple and they may be in for disappointment when they find there are no openings in the kind of career they chose.

There are those who may find themselves doing something else and may even change their choice of career. They need to have the willingness to be willing to do what is necessary until the opportunity comes along where they can start filling the dream they studied so hard for.

It is the willingness deep within each person as to how they handle their particular situation. It is so easy to sit back and wait for the right job to come along and when it does the sitting back feels so good that the job is passed by. The willingness to be willing to do what it takes to support one's self or one's family, not only builds confidence in one's self but also adds to the integrity and inner satisfaction that is the food for the soul and helps to bring about the good in one's experience.

A good example of this willingness is Kurt Warner who worked in a grocery store as a stock boy and a year later won the Superbowl. Kurt knew he was a good football player and was willing to do what was necessary until the opportunity came to him. He was willing to do something until the time was right to move forward with what he loved to do.

While working at the store, Kurt met a person who later became his wife and together they have a program that helps the special needs children throughout the country and abroad.

That may be the reason Kurt worked at the store so that the Creative Force of the Universe (God) could put the two of them together to do the work they are doing for the special needs children. God knows what needs to be done before the plan is put into the minds of the people involved. When one allows the inner feeling to guide the everyday activities, it can make life a pleasure and joy because it is God expressing through us, as us.

There are times when the blocks that hold the good from coming forward have to be removed so the good thoughts and ideas can come through. Removing the blocks is part of the willingness to be willing to do what it takes to let life unfold in Divine Order and recognize the good when it comes about.

I see the life of these new graduates moving forward in their careers because they are willing to be willing to listen to the small still voice within and act on the ideas that come to them. There is no reason for any of them to sit around and do nothing because there is something for everyone when one is willing.

And So It Is

CHANGES

*In all thy ways acknowledge Him,
and He shall direct thy paths. Proverbs 3:6*

There are people working jobs and doing their every day activities who are creating a lot of worry, fear and depression in their life because of their attitudes. When a person is working a job they do not like, they jeopardize their health, their relationships with others, and their ability to be productive to their fullest. It is the performance on the job that a boss looks at when it is time for a raise in pay or a promotion to a higher position.

Getting up in the morning and going to a job you dislike creates a lot of disharmony throughout the whole day. It brings about stress, fear, and a lot of unnecessary worry which can lead to a state of deep depression.

If every person were working a job they really liked then most companies would not have to have a sick leave policy in their operation. The production loss each day by companies across this nation is at a very high level because there are so many people working jobs they do not like.

To find a job you like, the first thing is to figure out what you would love to do. When you ask for help from the Creative Force of the Universe (God) then you will find out what you should be doing to create joy and harmony in your life.

When we trust God to guide and direct us, then we are impelled to new adventures. The inner security we feel takes us along the right path in the work we were guided to seek. When we remember that there is something greater than we are that dwells within and we can use that something to guide us in making the right decision, then we are on the right track to a life of joy, harmony and love.

By changing our attitude about our present job we can bring about peace of mind and relieve the worry and stress we put ourselves through. When we ask God for help in overcoming any experience that is causing worry and fear, then we are calling on that something that dwells within and we get that inner feeling that all is well.

Ernest Holmes writes, "God is forever doing new things, and when we conceive new ideas, it is an act of the indwelling presence of God projecting Itself into creation." What he is saying is the thoughts and ideas we get are the guidance of God expressing through us as us.

The new job you want can be yours when you call on God for what you love to do, and follow through on the thoughts and ideas that come to you. Only you can do it for you when you trust the guidance from "that something" that dwells in the center of our being which I know is a loving and giving God.

And So It Is

The Divine Pattern

Be Perfect, be of good comfort, be of one mind, live in peace; and the God of love and peace shall be with you.
II Corinthians 13:11

I refuse to think of all the confusion it would cause to man if he planted an acorn and instead of an oak tree he would get a pine tree. We all know there is no way that kind of a situation could happen. Within that acorn is an invisible pattern of what the tree is to look like and also in that acorn is a divine pattern of what the tree is to do after it becomes a tree.

The divine pattern in that tree gives it the ability to produce more acorns. Within everything that has been created is the divine pattern of what it is to do. By reproducing what it is keeps the abundance of the Universe flowing. It is not just the trees and plants that have this divine pattern in them, it is every living thing on this planet.

There is an invisible plan for every living thing and that includes man. There is a divine pattern for each of us and within the pattern for good we have the freedom to unfold. Just as there is an invisible pattern for our body, so also for our life there is an invisible Divine Pattern of perfection and fulfillment. Our awareness that such a pattern exists enables us to harmonize our desires with it.

Know within yourself the desires you want in your life, such as, what you want to become, where you want to live, and what you want to achieve. This true knowledge of what you want, your desire, is indispensable for giving direction to your life, for when we dwell consciously on what we want, we then attract that to ourselves.

Jesus said "it is done unto you as you believe" and when you truly believe in what your desires are then this invisible force of the Universe puts things in motion to create your desires. There are people who write out their desires every day and that keeps their desires very strong in their consciousness. When you set your intention and focus your thoughts on that intention then it is attracted to you. The daily writing and thinking leaves a deep impression on the subconscious mind and out of those impressions comes the realization of our desires, spiritual growth, health, happiness, prosperity, protection and fulfillment.

The Divine Pattern of your life unfolds for you when you stay balanced in mind body and spirit. Allow the loving God that dwells within you to guide you in your everyday activities and the peace and joy in your life is unlimited.

And So It Is

TRANSFORMATION—THE WAY TO YOUR GOOD

Do not imitate the way of the world, but be transformed by the renewing of your mind. Romans 12:2

There are a lot of things changing at this time of the year here in this beautiful valley we enjoy so much. I travel a lot of miles each week and I see so many things changing from what they were three months ago. Most of the bounty from the vines and trees have been harvested and added to the abundance that the Creative Force of the Universe (God) has created for mankind. We watch God in action as the leaves on the broad leaf trees start to change color and create the beauty that is so wonderful to look at.

This time of year, when I lived back east, was always a time of beauty everywhere you traveled. The Skyline Drive in Virginia was always bumper to bumper with traffic observing the beauty of the Blue Ridge Mountains with the array of color from the different kinds of trees that covered the mountains. Viewing the valley from the top of the Blue Ridge Mountains was a sight you could never forget. God sure paints a beautiful picture at this time of the year in every part of this wonderful country we enjoy.

Every living thing is going through the transformation process in order to prepare for the coming cycle of production next season. The trees will take on a new look when the leaves drop and the pruners move through cutting out the branches that have served their purpose. The vines will also take on a new look for the same reason.

The transformation process that a tree or vine goes through is not much different than the transformation process that man goes through when he finally realizes who and what he really is and what his purpose on this planet really is.

The indwelling presence of God in man is the guiding system of the thoughts we get. The action we take on those thoughts is always for our best and highest good when we get quiet and listen for what should be done.

The transformation man goes through is by his choice and has nothing to do with the change of seasons. As the tree sheds its leaves, man must shed the negative thoughts in his mind. Get rid of judging, resentment, jealousy, anger and lying. Replace all of the above with unconditional love and harmony toward all living things.

In order to transform your life, you cannot lie to yourself about your feelings. You have to get rid of the deadwood in your tree of life and prune out anything that is holding you back from the life you want to live. The choice is yours and nobody outside of you can do it for you.

To be "born again" you renew your mind by going through the transformation process getting rid of what is not serving you because it is only holding you back from your good. Life is beautiful when you ask God to paint your picture of life, and see that beauty in all other beings on this planet.

And So It Is

Passion—An Overwhelming Desire

*Men what are you doing? We also are ordinary
human beings like you. Acts 14:15*

I know several people doing the thing they love to do and getting great joy from it. While talking to some of these people I found out they were doing something they had always wanted to do and were now at a time in their life when they could do it. A lot of people have a desire for something, but do not have a passion for it.

There is a lot of difference between having a desire and a passion. With a desire you just let life unfold and if the desire you have happens to be in that part of the unfoldment, then your "wish" has come true. When you wish for something you desire and it doesn't come about, then you feel that it wasn't meant to be for you. Most people go through their whole life wishing for things and never understanding that by having a passion for something they could attract it into their life.

When you have a passion for something, whether it be some material thing or just a better understanding of who you are, then it will happen in the way you expect. That may sound a little confusing to some people, but those who understand realize that what you focus your mind on with feeling is what you get. In other words, change your thinking, change your life. Jesus said "as a man thinketh in his heart so is he," I interpret that quote from the Bible as, change your thinking, change your life.

When you have a passion for something in your life, and know how to focus your mind on what it is you want, then you will attract that into your life. The passion you have for it cannot be detoured away from the forefront of your mind if you really want what you feel the passion for.

You can attract what you desire if you keep your mind focused on your desire and have a passion for it. I have had things come into my life because I had an overwhelming desire for somethings that showed up in my experience.

These things happened before I was introduced to the Science of Mind teaching. As I learn about this teaching, I no longer do wishful thinking, because I now know I can have whatever I want by directing my thoughts toward it and being passionate about it. It may take some time for it to become form or a reality in my life because God works out the time for it to unfold.

I have all I need to live a very fulfilling life and no longer wish for the things I want. I allow the Father within to direct my thoughts, and the action I take on those thoughts are always for my best and highest good. Every being on this planet is capable of having everything they need because every being is created equal and all have the same power within to attract whatever they want.

Don't be a wishful thinker, know what you want, be passionate about it, let go and let God handle the details of having it show up in your experience. God is good when you open up and allow it.

And So It Is

GIVE PRAISE

Let the heavens and the earth praise Him, the seas, and everything that moves therein. Psalms 69:34

It gives me a delightful feeling to see the results of the different age baseball teams published in the Madera Tribune. So many papers publish the "news" but it seems to be all the negative news. It is difficult for me to understand why negative news sells more papers than positive news. It seems to me that everyone is looking for the "bad" in every story.

The young people on these ball teams should have all the praise that can be mustered because they are of the age when a lot of them find out they are somebody and that other people care. So many people at that age come to a fork in their road of life and without praise and feeling other people care, usually take the fork that leads to not so good results. Even if one chooses the fork that leads to a not so good situation, there is still time to turn that person's thoughts around by giving praise, for a job well done, and letting them know they are somebody. To plant the seed thoughts in a young person's mind that they can do and be whatever they choose to be, can build self-esteem and bring out the talents they didn't realize they had.

I was so blessed while growing up to have a father who understood that I had to make my own choices. There were chores to be done on the farm that we were instructed on, but something for my own personal desire, I was never told what or how to do it. When I made a personal mistake, my father would tell me to think about something a little longer before making a choice, and he didn't tell me I was dumb, stupid, and would never amount to anything.

I had a good friend in high school who lived his life under those kind of abusive comments. He was never allowed to make any choices of his own because his father was very controlling and didn't trust him to do anything for himself. He didn't drive a car because his father didn't want to teach him to drive because he might wreck the family car.

He didn't receive any praise for any of the good deeds he did, so as soon as he graduated from high school he joined the military.

I lost contact with him but did see his father a few years later and he told me where Mike was and what he was doing. It surprised me to hear his father say that he didn't trust Mike with a $500 family car, but the U.S. Government now trusts him with a five million dollar jet airplane. He was a very good student with high grades in school, but was never allowed to be on his own or make any choices for himself until he got away from his controlling father.

It is okay to let a young person be a young person, and give them praise for deeds well done and when a mistake is made be there for them. To be there for them in a time of need builds trust in them and helps them form their mind, to think before they leap. Give them plenty of praise and you might be surprised about what they become.

And So It Is

Build "Your" Field of Dreams

Be transformed by the renewing of your mind.
Romans 12:2

The Law of Attraction is starting to show up in all sorts of publications and several television networks. There are those who don't pay much attention to what the books are saying or the programs that have been produced by the different networks to get the information out to those they can help. There was a time in my life when I would not have given a book or program on the subject a second thought. Things in my life then were unfolding as I was "expecting."

It was not until I saw the movie <u>Field of Dreams</u> that I had given much thought as to how things were drawn into my life by the way I thought. There were material things showing up in my life that I was "expecting" because they were part of my goals. It wasn't until I found the Science of Mind teaching that it all made sense as to why things manifest in one's life when he or she sets their intentions on what they want. It worked for me even before I understood how the Law of Attraction worked as a mind connection with the Creative Force of the Universe (God).

The Science of Mind teaching gave me a powerful understanding as to why, in the movie they said "if you build it they will come." I thought back about the goals I set and the material things showing up in my life because they were what I was thinking about.

The term "change your thinking and change your life" is not something new because the Buddha and the great teacher Jesus related to the same thing. In Proverbs 23:7 Jesus said "as a man thinketh in his heart so is he" is about the same as "if you build it they will come" in the movie <u>Field of Dreams</u>.

When I lived and worked back East, there were people I worked with that considered me very lucky to get the things I had by setting goals and seeing them show up. I was able to buy them because of the job I had by setting a goal for it.

The job I had was what I always wanted because being a mechanic is what I loved to do. I didn't know anything about the Law of Attraction at that time but I see now that it will work for anyone whether one understands it or not.

The movie <u>The Secret</u>, that has swept the country and the world is all about how the Law of Attraction works when one sets a goal or sets his or her intention on something specific that they want to manifest in their life. It is so great to be able to make a choice as to what I want in my life and what I don't want.

I set my intention on what it is I want and that sets the gears in motion for the Universal Law of Attraction to bring it or something better into my life. Some people think it is voodoo and don't pay any attention to what Jesus tried to teach when He said, "pray knowing that it is done unto you as you believe," which relates back to the movie <u>Field of Dreams</u> or "as a man thinketh so is he."

One has to do it for themselves because no one can do it for you. Only you have control over your mind so, change your thinking and change your life and build your own field of dreams.

And So It Is

Build on a Solid Foundation

He is like a wise man who builds his house upon a rock.
Matthew 7:24

There was a time in my life when I would try to take shortcuts in order to save time and labor. There were times when things worked out great and there were times when things didn't turn out to be so great. Those were the times when I wished I had taken the time to do it the way I was instructed. I never got into serious trouble from it but it had to be done right and that took much more time than if I had forgotten the shortcuts and followed the instructions.

I suppose everyone has a tendency to want to save time and money, so they do take a chance. When things turn out good and is noticed by others, it makes one feel that he or she made a wise decision and saved some time and money. On the other hand, had it not turned out to be so good and was noticed by others, then the feeling of defeat falls on one's mind and a lot of thought comes about as to why I didn't do it right to start with. The thought of "I should have done it the other way or I should have followed the instructions closer."

The thoughts one has about what one should have or should not have done, can drag one to a very low energy level and cause one to think they are not worthy. One's self-esteem is very important in making a decision and coping with the outcome should it be great or not so great.

One of the greatest feelings is to accept the outcome and not allow a not so good outcome to zap one's energy level. All mistakes should be considered a learning experience and then move on to whatever the next project is. When one dwells on the past experiences and tries to move on to a new experience it is like building a new building on an old foundation. Clear the mind of the past experience and build on a new solid foundation for the next project. When we can let go of the old experience and rely on it as a learning experience, then we are not putting new wine in old skins as Jesus said in Matthew 7:24. By putting the wine in a new skin one does not have to take a chance of it rupturing.

When one relies on the Creative Energy (God) that dwells within, then the foundation becomes solid and can withstand anything one builds on it. The trust and self esteem one has of themselves is the power of the presence within (God) guiding one's thoughts and building more trust and faith within themselves.

The trust and faith one has of the Creative Energy of the Universe (God) is a solid foundation one can build anything on and know in one's mind that it can stand forever. The faith and trust is what creates a life of joy, peace, love and harmony when one is open to receive.

And So It Is

March To The Beat of Your Own Drum

He that is slow to wrath is of great understanding.
Proverbs 14:29

While working back east I had a chance to meet many different people and many from different cultures. The way people lived their life was of interest to me because in growing up, life on the farm didn't include much change.

While in the military I met people from every part of this wonderful country. Some of the people were leaders and most of the others had to be led. The ones that had leader ability were of interest to me because I was eager to learn what was behind their thinking. The way they would look at a problem or a situation and the action they would take soon reflected their ability, whether they were leaders or needed to be led.

Each person is different and while working with different people, I soon learned that a self-motivated person was the most outgoing and was always looking for new opportunities. Those were the people who could tolerate a lot of verbal abuse before they raised their voice in protest.

The scripture at the beginning of this article refers to the word wrath; according to Webster, wrath means anger or punishment. Those who are in full control of their lives do not get angry or try to punish others. To them life is for living and to get the most out of every day they are calm when they are in contact with other people.

People need people in order to cope with situations in life and to find the answers to what they should do to create the joy life has to offer. A person learns that anger only creates more anger and that can lead to an out of control situation.

The peace and harmony that comes into ones everyday experience is the Creative Force of the Universe (God) expressing It's love out of Itself for everyone to enjoy. How one handles the good that comes his or her way is a reflection of how they think.

To recognize the good in life one has to be open in one's thinking and allow the good thoughts to blank out all of the negativity. The good thoughts are the thoughts that bring the feeling of self-control and that builds self-confidence. Self-confidence is what keeps a self motivated person in a happy state of mind and he or she knows they can do anything.

Those are the people who plan their life around what they think and the action he or she takes always has the expected results.

When a person makes plans for what they want their life to be and they "march to the beat of their own drum," then life unfolds in a way that creates the joy, peace, harmony and love that we were created to experience.

And So It Is

Share In All of Nature and In All Good

Let us not love in word, neither in tongue;
but in deed and the truth. I John 3:18

I am always amazed when I see the acts of some of the animals and the birds of God's Kingdom. It is such a joy for me to sit on my patio and watch the activities of the birds in my backyard. I always put out feed for them and I have several kinds of birds enjoying the food.

There is a pair of bluebirds that are very aggressive toward the others. When the others are eating, the bluebirds will sail in and scare the others away but they soon return when the blue-birds leave.

I noticed that fewer and fewer of the birds were com-ing to the food but the bluebirds were always in the area. I saw that the bluebirds were build-ing a nest in one of the trees close to my house. They would get very aggressive toward any bird that came into the back-yard and soon they claimed ownership of the whole place.

When the crows would take their bath when the sprinklers were on, the bluebirds would dive at them until the crows would finally leave. There aren't any birds coming for food be-cause the bluebirds will not allow it. I don't know whether it is the fear of the bluebirds or the respect the other birds have of the bluebirds territory. What-ever it is, is working, because the bluebirds have the whole backyard to themselves.

Watching all of this take place over the last month and a half has made me wonder how many of us would quit coming to the feedbox because of some aggressive person try-ing to control the portions we get. It might work in the bird and animal kingdom but not in the part of the animal kingdom that includes man.

Man is an expression of God in action and knows that in order to live a life in Truth, as the scripture says, one needs to share the good deeds that bring a very satisfied feeling. In so doing the more one gives, the more one has to share and is able to spread the good deed out to many others. Man has more ways to survive than some of the other animals and birds because man has choice.

I am anxious to see what happens when the young bluebirds leave the nest and the wall of defense comes down. I feel it is a silent way the bluebirds have to let others know that it is their territory and no one is welcome. It will be interesting to see the end results.

I know the good deeds man does, not only for his fellow man but for the animals on this planet, are the way of getting the spiritual food one needs in order to satisfy the inner feeling of the soul. The spiritual food is needed if one is to live a life in the "Truth" all beings were created to live. Enjoy the birds and animals for what they are but feed the soul within with good deeds.

And So It Is

THE INFINITE INTELLIGENCE IN ALL SEEDS

I have planted, Apollo watered; but God gave the increase.
I Corinthians 3:6

While living back East, I always raised a big garden for our vegetables and other summer food. I had several apple trees, peach trees, plum trees and some apricot trees. It was always a joy to see the trees bloom, get the ground ready to plant the garden and get dirt under my fingernails.

At that time I didn't give much thought about what had to happen in the Universe for the trees to bloom or the garden to thrive. As I grew older and found the Science of Mind teaching, then it all made sense as to how the Creative Intelligence of the Universe (God) works through everything that one can see, taste, touch, smell and hear.

I have a better understanding of how this Creative Intelligence is in every seed that is planted and in every tree that blooms and bears its fruit and nuts. The seeds of all vegetation on this planet have this Intelligence within and knows when and what to do in God's time.

My neighbor always got his garden in about two to three weeks before I could find time to get mine planted. I always had green beans, squash and other vegetables before he did. The reason for this was in the God timing of the seeds. My neighbor would put his garden in when the soil was not warm enough for the seeds to germinate.

The temperature of the soil was warm when I put my garden in and the Intelligence in the seeds knew it was time to sprout. I did not realize this until I had a better understanding of the Creative Intelligence that is around us, for us, and through everything on this planet. Man can use this Creative Intelligence a little different than the seeds one puts in the ground or the Intelligence in the trees that bloom and bear fruit. When one plants corn seeds, one gets a corn stalk that bears ears of corn. Once the corn sprouts there is no turning back on what it is to become.

Once man plants seed thoughts in his mind and the Law of Attraction starts to manifest what the thoughts are to produce and man does not like what is manifesting, then he can change his thoughts and change what is manifesting. A corn seed cannot do that because it has one purpose and that is to grow a corn stalk that produces ears of corn.

With man's mind connected to the One Mind of the Universe, and with man being able to think and make choices, then the Creative Intelligence that is in everything is what one should allow to guide his or her life. Only good can come to one who uses this Creative Process and trusts It to the fullest to guide one's everyday activities. The life one lives is a reflection of how much one uses this Creative Intelligence (God) in his or her everyday activities.

And So It Is

Don't Trust Your Perception

Through faith we understand that the worlds were framed by the word of God. Hebrews 11:3

The perception of a situation we form in our minds may not be what one might think it to be. The understanding of what took place is always the truth of the situation when one trusts Spirit for the truth to come through.

I know it might sound confusing because the perception I have in my mind may not be what others have seen and formed their perception from. Two people can witness the same action of others and not be able to agree on what really took place. It is the perception one forms in one's mind that the stories are built from.

When one is dealing with children it is very important that one has a good understanding of what took place. A child may think he or she is doing something that would please a parent, teacher or mentor and it may turn out to be something that hurts that child if the perception of the situation is made without the understanding of what the child was trying to express.

It is so important that the person in charge does not express his or her feelings about the situation and say something out of frustration or anger that can hurt someone else, especially a child. It only takes one comment or word to a child, at a time of frustration, and that comment or word is carried by that child into adulthood.

In some of the classes we conduct at our Center, there are people who tell about things that were said to them when they were a child and it has been a part of them their whole life. It takes some work on their part to clear their minds of what they had been carrying because of what was said to them as a child.

A young mind is like a sponge and soaks up all that is said whether it be one word or a comment. A word can cut deeper than a sword and can cause hurt for a lifetime. The wound from a sword can heal and sometimes not leave a scar, but the wound from a word may never heal and can inflict hurt for a lifetime.

The things parents say to their children can bring hurt for a lifetime or can lift them up in self-esteem and help them overcome any negative situation they may be faced with while growing up. The more good things a parent, teacher or mentor can say to a child, the more they will embody them and the more self-confidence the child will have.

There should never be a destructive word or comment used in the discipline of a child because that is the time when the child will embody all that is said and chances are they will carry it for the rest of their life.

We all want our children to be the best and have the best so why not give them the best in the way of encouragement and respect. Make positive comments about their looks, the way they dress, and how quickly they learn, because they are our future. Allow Spirit to reveal the understanding.

And So It Is

DIFFICULTIES WILL BE OVERCOME

It is your Father's good pleasure to give you the Kingdom.
Luke 12:32

There are times when a person may think there is no end to the problems that keep jumping up in one's everyday experiences. A friend of mine back east was always trying to overcome some problem that seemed to happen every day. He was a good person, worked with integrity, and could be counted on for any assignment given to him. His family knew they could depend on him for any support they needed.

He had two sons in their early twenties that were carbon copies of their father and it was a joy for me to be in their company. My friend did not attend any church except for special events. I was the same way in my church attendance but I didn't have as many difficulties as he had in his everyday activities.

There was a time in his life when things were normal and he was always busy with his family and having fun. He told me stories of the things he did with his family and how much he enjoyed doing them.

After the boys left home and were on their own was when his life started to become a life full of problems and difficulties. I didn't know at the time what to tell him to do because I didn't know. As I think back over the time we spent working together I can now understand why his life was full of problems.

He was always used to taking care of his family and now there was no one who needed his support. In his mind he created these problems so he would have something to do and that was to help himself. That may sound far fetched, but it happens to a person when things change in their life and they don't change with the change that is taking place in their life.

In Donald Curtis' book, <u>How To Be Great</u>, he writes about overcoming difficulties. He writes that the most important part is for one to recognize that the indwelling presence of Spirit is the answer to overcoming any problem and leads to a life full of peace and joy. When one goes outside of one's self to find the answers then one creates more problems. The answers are at the center of our being because that is the place of the Most High which is the secret closet Jesus referred to.

When we raise our consciousness to a higher level and call upon the Spirit within for guidance, then we get the answers. I didn't realize this at the time when my friend was having his problems, so I was unable to help him.

Every being on this planet creates the life they live by the way they think. The problems that come into our life can be solved very easily when one goes within one's own secret closet and allows the Spirit within to guide one's everyday activities. To God there are no impossible difficulties and being one with God, we have no difficulties.

And So It Is

SEE THE PEACE AND HARMONY IN YOUR LIFE

Be of the same mind one toward another.
Romans 12:16

During my high school days, I was amazed at the different people that we had in our class. I was used to a one room school with the same people in the neighborhood. It was quite an experience for me to adjust to high school in order to be part of the group.

I remember a fellow on our football team that could see the good in any situation and have fun regardless of how rough the going was. His name was Richard and we became friends the first week of practice. There were those who didn't care for Richard because he was always happy and a joy to have in the group.

I learned, as time went on, that those who didn't care much for Richard didn't care much for anybody. They were so wrapped up in themselves that there was no room for anyone else in their space. Needless to say those people didn't do very well on the football team or in the classroom.

It took some time on my part to figure out it was their attitude about life that was keeping them in their own little world. They didn't try to reach out to anyone and of course no one tried to reach toward them.

I had some wonderful teachers who explained to me that the reason some people stay in their own space was because they have a fear of being turned down or hurt. I was taught at home that if I reached first, I would get a response from whomever I tried to reach. I didn't always get the response I expected but it broke the ice and made the next time much easier for them to express. As Abraham Lincoln said, "a person is as happy as they make up their minds to be."

Richard and I stayed friends all through high school and for some time after we graduated. He joined the Army because his older brother was in the Army and I lost contact with him. I am sure, while in the Army, his happy go lucky attitude created a lot of friends for him. So many people go through life trying to do everything themselves and they end up with a very lonely life.

As far back as I can remember I tried to live my life by the Golden Rule and in every situation it was very rewarding. After finding the Science of Mind teaching, I found I could relate to a lot of the things in the teaching because that was how I tried to live my life as an adult. I never allowed guilt, hatred, jealousy, or resentment to enter in any of the relationships I created with other people or when joining as a member of a group. The Science of Mind teaching is a reflection of my feelings while I was growing up and now, since I am a part of the teaching, it reinforces my awareness even more.

We were created to live a life of joy, peace and harmony and our attitude is the key to what we create our life to be. With an attitude of goodness and service to others, then we have fulfilled our mission of life on this planet. Change your thinking, change your life. Let go and let God show you the way.

And So It Is

WHEN SEARCHING FOR GUIDANCE, TRUST INTUITION

You shall seek me, and find me, when you search for me
with all your heart. Jeremiah 29:13

There are days when it is difficult to accomplish the things one plans to do. There are unexpected issues that jump up in one's face that take away from what was planned for the day. I know from experience that some issues have to be taken care of before one can move on to what was planned.

As a mechanic repairing heavy machinery there were times when my plans were disrupted because of other problems found while making the repairs that had to be corrected before I could finish the job. When the construction job has a deadline to meet, then each piece of equipment has to be in operating condition for the company to meet the schedule they set for the job to be completed.

When a machine was down, the superintendent on the job was concerned as to how long it would take to repair and if I gave him a time and then found something else that needed to be repaired it created a problem not only for me but the superintendent as well. That was why I learned not to set a specific time as to when the job would be completed because of the unexpected problems that might be found.

It is the same with all occupations, not only in the mechanic field. It creates a lot of stress on the person responsible and that can lead to a build up of anxiety that can take its toll on the physical body. I learned that if I stopped and allowed my mind to settle and not think about the problem, then things seemed to smooth out. I didn't know it at the time but it was a form of meditation that I now use in my every day activities when I need to solve a problem.

Every being has a built in guidance system that can be used to help solve the daily issues that jump up in one's face. It is called intuition and can be activated by stopping, get the mind quiet, and allowing the Creative Force of the Universe (God) to help bring one the answer needed.

I now understand and know why it works when one quiets the mind and gives the Father within the time to do the work. I see now that it was intuition that led me to stop, let my mind settle, then the job didn't seem to be as difficult as it first looked to be.

I know now, since being in Religious Science for over 20 years, that I create everything in my life by the way I think and the action I take. The mind we use every day to think with and to make decisions with, is an extension of the One Mind which is the Creative Force of the Universe (God).

When one is searching for guidance to solve an issue that is creating an unpleasant experience, that is the time he or she should get quiet and listen to the small still voice within, because that is the built in guidance system of God in action.

The thoughts and feelings one gets leads to the answer one is looking for when one can trust and believe their intuition. This is the built in protection system every being is created with, and is the extension of the God Mind that everyone uses each time one thinks and uses in the action one takes.

I know everyone is searching for ways to have a more joyous life and freedom. Focus on God and you are given the Kingdom.

And So It Is

Live Life in Truth, Not Confusion

Stand fast, and hold the traditions which you have been taught.
2 Thessalonians 2:15

The things we were taught while growing up were the guidelines one should live his or her life by. Some were very much misleading, but most were the right guidelines to live a happy and fruitful life. The families that prayed together were the families that seemed to enjoy life the most. I didn't realize it at the time, but it was touching on the innermost part of who we are.

I know now that every living creature on this planet uses the one mind of the universe (the Creative Intelligence, God) to live its life by. The different fowl use the one mind through its own mind to know when to migrate South and what direction to fly in. The animals that hibernate know when to prepare and find a place to spend the winter where they are sure to survive.

I know man doesn't fly South without an airplane and man doesn't have to find a place to hibernate for the winter months in order to survive. In order for man to survive and make the right choices, he or she depends on intuition. In the animals and other living things, there is another word for it, but it means the same thing, and that is instinct.

The difference is that man is able to think and make choices while the other living things just follow their feelings at the time. With man being able to make choices about the intuitive feelings he or she gets, sometimes adds confusion to one's life.

I know now that the teaching I got while growing up made my decision making a lot easier. I was taught to respect other people, don't lie, cheat or steal and to go on my "gut-feeling" when I had to make a choice. I know now that the gut feeling was the Creative Intelligence within me guiding my decision on what choice to make. It all makes so much more sense now than it did when I was growing up.

The Science of Mind teaching I have been associated with the past twenty plus years has opened my eyes and mind to what a joy life can be when one allows the guidance of Spirit within to give the answers when making a choice. There are those who call on others for their opinion before they can make a personal choice. This adds confusion to one's life and that brings about disharmony, struggle, fear, resentment, judgment of others, and all the other things that bring about a life full of disharmony.

I know all people were not taught the same while growing up. One can change the disharmony to a life of joy and harmony when one listens to the " Father within." I know a person's life will change when they listen to the intuitive voice. There is no room for confusion in one's life when one lives the truth of who he or she is — after all we are all God expressing.

And So It Is

The Egypt Consciousness Keeps One In Bondage

*And you shall know the truth
and the truth shall set you free. John 8:32*

The story of the children of Israel being in bondage in Egypt and how they were set free is a story one could relate to his or her life today. In the study of metaphysics it is a story of the soul moving from bondage to freedom as told in allegory in the book of Exodus in the Bible.

The Israelites were living in bondage in Egypt and were longing to return to their homeland. The metaphysical story relates to what can be applied to today's life so that a person can bring themselves out of the bondage of whatever is holding them down. Spiritual understanding is what can bring a person from bondage to freedom through a higher level of consciousness.

In the metaphysical story the word "Moses" means, "to draw out from" and the word "Egypt" means, "darkness, ignorance, pain and suffering." "Pharoah" means "the bondage of the world of appearances."

When one recognizes the oneness with the wisdom and guidance of Spirit, one can overcome the "Pharoah" consciousness and be set free from the bondage that is holding one back. One has to recognize what it is that causes the "Pharoah" consciousness and change whatever it is to a "Moses" consciousness in order to be drawn from the bondage that holds one back.

The thoughts one has and the action one takes is what creates the bondage and that can keep one from the good one seeks. Every being on this planet should be living a life free of fear, struggle and worry. It is the "Pharoah" thoughts one gets that keeps one in bondage. To react to the negative thoughts can only create more negativity in one's life. Allowing Spirit within to express wisdom and guidance through you is the "Moses" way of overcoming the "Pharoah" consciousness.

There are so many disruptions in one's daily life that it is difficult to separate all the negative from the positive. A thought can lead to what may seem the right path to take only to find out it was not the proper choice. That is okay because one can always change directions and look for the guidance from within to direct his or her course.

It is of our own creative thoughts that we build a life of joy and peace. It is the indwelling Presence of the Father that gives one the wisdom and guidance to make the right choice. Staying out of the "Pharoah" consciousness and allowing the "Moses" consciousness to draw one out of the bondage thoughts will give one freedom.

When one raises in consciousness and takes charge of the life that is here to live, one does not have to bend to anyone's will in the outer part of one's world. The will of the Father is the one true will or the will of God is the will of life.

By allowing the will of God to flow through our everyday life, then the "Pharoah" consciousness of bondage has a difficult time trying to enter one's thoughts. One can move from the land of darkness and bondage and into the promise land of true freedom when one listens to the Father within and follows the thoughts one gets.

And So It Is

The Reward of Accepting Yourself
The desire accomplished is sweet to the Soul.
Proverbs 13:19

There was a time in my life where I thought that in order to live a good life I had to work hard and make a lot of money. I did that from the time I got out of the military in 1953 until 1988 after moving to California in 1979. My day was to start early and work late in order to keep everybody happy. I thought I had to satisfy everyone else and that how I felt didn't matter.

I had a neighbor, when I lived in Ohio, who was always helping everyone in the neighborhood including myself. He had a home business and had a lot of free time, so he would find things to do for the people in the neighborhood. In the winter he would get up early and give me a hand shoveling snow from my driveway so I could get my truck out of the barn and go to work. I appreciated the help and let him know how much it helped me out. All he would say was "I enjoy being of service to anyone who needs a hand."

What I didn't understand at the time was that he was satisfying the inner self by helping others. He was bringing the outer self in balance with the inner self as Ralph Waldo Emerson explains in some of his writings.

Emerson says, "our purpose is to bring the two selves together, for they are potentially the same and can express as one." I understand that now, but back in Ohio that was the farthest thing from my mind because I was too busy making a living to have thoughts like that enter my mind.

Most people are living in that kind of consciousness and don't want to hear about the inner feeling being the biggest part of their life. It is all part of accepting yourself and allowing the inner feeling (God) to keep one balanced in inner and outer feelings. The inner feeling is always perfect, the outer feeling is potentially perfect.

When one is separated in consciousness from the higher inner self (God) then one is opening up to the outer development of conflict, struggle, tension, false appearances, unhappiness and that is the cause of most illnesses.

When one listens to the feeling of the inner voice, then he or she can make the choice to make the outer feeling match the inner feeling. It is all part of accepting oneself to be the greatest in any activity and to love oneself for who and what he or she is. Every being on this planet has the same amount of the God stuff in them and it is what they do with it that brings out the self acceptance of themselves. My neighbor in Ohio knew and understood this and that is why he was loved and accepted by all who knew him.

After being in the Science of Mind teaching for the past 20 or so years, I now make it a natural part of my life to keep the inner and the outer feelings balanced. Doing so creates a life of joy, peace, harmony, love, and acceptance of myself and everyone I come in contact with. Any desire I accomplish makes the inner soul happy and that in turn creates an outer life that is full of happiness, love and peace.

And So It Is

Expectation Awakens The Power Within

Nothing shall be impossible unto you.
Matthew 17:20

There is a power within that is waiting to be called upon, but most people are unaware of Its existence. This power is what Jesus referred to as the Father within. This same power keeps the planets in orbit, keeps the sun shining, and the production of all the abundance we share on this planet.

There are those who think they have to do everything in order to survive. That was my way of thinking, until it was explained to me that I was part of this power and that this power would work for me if I worked it. To a lot of people that may sound far fetched, but it is true if one believes what Jesus taught. Jesus said "it is not I but the Father within who does the work."

The power within is the presence of the Creative Force of the Universe (God) and is our divine birthright. This divine birthright consists of all of God's wisdom, all of God's life, all of God's love, all of God's wholeness, and all of God's power.

When one lives a life full of expectations, with everything one does, the power within is awakened. When one prays or uses positive affirmations in a part of his or her daily life, then the power within, that has been waiting to serve, is awakened and good things start happening to the one with the expectations.

When a person stumbles through life, accepting only what falls his or her way and doesn't expect anything great to happen in their life, then it won't. One should always expect the best of everything to happen to them. When one's focus is on the good things in life, then the power within goes into action to create what is needed to bring about what he or she expects. With high expectations and belief in the power within, then there isn't anything a person can't do or be.

There are people who are always waiting for their good to show up and have no idea that it is how they think that brings about their good. The attitude one has about themselves is pictured in the kind of life they are living. Thoughts are things and one's life and the things that happen are a result of how one thinks. Man's life is a result of how and what he is thinking and the power within creates according to his thinking.

There are times when something happens that one doesn't expect, but whatever it was is a signal to think about what one is thinking about. A person can change anything in their life by changing the way they think. When one keeps high expectations as the focus of his or her thoughts, the power within is always at work bringing about what one expects. As for ourselves we can do nothing; it is the Father within that does whatever is needed to bring about the expectations.

Keep the power within awake at all times by expecting the best of everything to happen in your life and to all others in your experience. It is a great life when you expect it to be.

And So It Is.

Honor Yourself

Wist ye not that I must be about my Father's business.
Luke 2:49

I was traveling with a friend in the Midwest on a trip that would keep us together for several days. We were coming into a small town just at lunch time and were ready for some lunch and a stretch of the legs. When we found a small restaurant with plenty of parking, we decided it would be the place to have lunch.

When we got out of the car, a young man approached us with a bucket and cleaning materials and asked to clean our windshield and side windows. Since it was my friend's car, he gave the young man five dollars to do the job. The young man was so delighted with the five dollars, he said to my friend, it would be what he needed to buy his mother a bouquet of flowers since she was coming home from the hospital after major surgery that could save her life. My friend felt good that he could contribute to a worthwhile cause, and we went into the restaurant.

After being seated, the waitress came to take our order and my friend asked the cost of ham and an order of toast. The waitress said it would be five dollars and my friend said he would pass and just have coffee. I needed something to eat and told my friend to go for the ham and toast because lunch was on me. His eyes brightened up and we enjoyed a nice lunch.

After lunch I asked him why he would give the young man in the parking lot five dollars and then not pay five dollars for something he wanted for himself. He said it seemed a little too much for what it was and he didn't feel it was worth it. It left me a little confused about his way of thinking and I asked him why he didn't think he was worth the five dollars to get what he wanted.

He did not have an answer and we talked about self worth

of ourselves. His idea was that the young man in the parking lot was willing to work for the payment made to him. I felt it was well and good, but what about self worth being the first order of service. In order to serve the Father within, it is okay to help the neighbor in the parking lot, but what about the self? Jesus said, "love thy neighbor as thy self," which to me means love thyself before passing good or love to the neighbor.

There are so many people depriving themselves from the abundance of the Universe because of an attitude and feeling he or she has about themselves. It is no doubt that the intent to help others gives them a good feeling, but it is the self service that feeds the inner soul and keeps the spirit alive within.

I have read stories, dating back before Jesus to the modern day time, that the inner soul needs the same amount of nourishment that the physical body needs in order to function. The spiritual body within needs prayer, meditation and the understanding of one's self worth in order to serve each being with his or her good. It is the Father within that one can call on when there is a problem in the outer world that needs to be addressed. The outer world around each being depends upon the inner feelings about the Father within.

What one does to feed the inner feeling with spiritual nourishment depends on the attitude they have of themselves. All problems can be answered when one understands the spiritual part of themselves. Love thyself and allow the Father within to take care of the details for a life of joy, peace and harmony.

And So It Is

THE COURAGE TO MOVE FORWARD

Nothing in life is to be feared. It is only to be understood.
Marie Curie

I was channel surfing and tuned in to the Discovery Channel and there was a documentary on the Loggerhead Turtle. The studies that have been made by biologists and scientists on this great creature were very interesting to me. Anything that is of the way nature works is the way God expresses Itself to let us know that all is good because everything is God expressing.

The Loggerhead Turtle endures a lot of hardship in order to continue to exist as it has for millions of years. It leaves the shores of Mexico for the long journey to the place where it lays its eggs and reproduces itself hundreds of times over. The journey is about 9100 miles from Mexico to Wake Island where she will lay her eggs and leave to return to Mexico to start the journey next year.

During the journey she has to combat the storms of the seas, the predators looking for food, and be able to find enough food for her to survive herself. She can dive a mile deep, along with the sperm whale, to get the squid that live at that level in the Western Atlantic Ocean. It is a long and dangerous journey for her and she uses the temperature of the water for her guide. The different currents of the ocean, from what I understand, is the way she knows she is going in the right direction.

The animals, birds and sea life are all created with a built in system for the survival of each species. The hardships some animals endure is difficult to understand, but there is a reason for it. They have no fear of what they have to do and for man to understand this is reason enough to study the habits of different species and learn all we can of how they survive. With man having the ability to think and make choices helps man through some of his hardships by changing the way he does things.

With the animals, birds and sea life it is all they know and they will keep on doing it without any changes. There are those people who feel they have to suffer and fear in order to live a full life with self-satisfaction. The Creative Intelligence of the Universe (God) created man out of love and man's life was never intended to suffer, fear, or experience lack and limitation.

The realization of the indwelling presence of this Creative Force at the center of our being, creates within each being what is needed to guide one to a life of joy, peace and harmony. The lilies of the field, they toil not and spin not and just be what they were created to be. With man being created out of love is reason enough to be love expressing at all times and the life of love creates more love into one's experience.

There is no reason to suffer and fear when we move forward with an understanding of the nature of man and how the Creative Force of the Universe (God) expresses through man by way of intuition. It is the small still voice within that keeps man guided in the right direction for the life that man was intended to live.

The understanding of who and what we are and what our purpose on this planet is can be the first step to a life of joy, peace and harmony. When one is open to receive the understanding through the small still voice within, then there should be no fear of moving forward with life.

And So It Is

WHEN DOES ONE FEEL MATURE?

Let this mind be in you, which was also in Christ Jesus.
Philippians 2:5

The mind mentioned in the scripture verse is being related to a mature mind or mature person. The level of consciousness that puts man's thinking at a higher level of knowing himself is a measure of maturity. The immaturity projected in the breakdown of moral, cultural, and social standards is an indication of a lower level of consciousness.

The high consciousness which brings peace, true love, inner security, confidence, pride, integrity and strength are all marks of a mature person. One may ask, how does one raise his or her level of consciousness? Every being was created with the same amount of "Christ Consciousness" and it is the person who seeks first the Kingdom that recognizes the power within and uses it.

There is no event outside of oneself that can do what the power within can do when a person calls on that power to help with a situation or a problem. The Creative Force of the Universe (God) is the source of all our good and one's awareness of that Source is the amount of good one receives. The more awareness, the higher the consciousness.

The ever growing consciousness is always changing as one integrates the personality with the divine individuality. The personality is made up of false ego as well as the true ego. The immaturity comes from the false ego. The false ego must be dissolved; the true ego, the divine individuality must be recognized as the strength and power each being has within.

By allowing the true ego to come forth and be recognized is a way to eliminate the false ego which can spoil any situation by causing some kind of conflict or unhappiness. When the spiritual consciousness is allowed to come forth and to be a guide for one's life, then one's life is filled with love, faith, beauty, dedication, honesty and peace.

There are times when the false ego shows up in one's life in the way of a problem or discomfort and can be turned away by seeking the Kingdom of God with thoughts of harmony, love and peace. The false ego will try to override the true ego; however, one's higher level of consciousness can always bring forth the true ego which is an outpicture of the mature person who uses the Christ within for guidance.

The growing up part of man is to allow the spiritual unfoldment in one's life, always choosing what is best for themselves and all others in the experience. The mature person has recognized the one mind of God being the only mind and each being uses that one mind each time he or she thinks or makes a decision.

The true ego is recognizing the Christ consciousness within and following the direction given by the small voice within. Seek first the Kingdom and all else comes with ease when one knows the truth of themselves.

And So It Is

THERE'S ALWAYS ENOUGH AT ALL TIMES

All things that the Father has are mine.
John 16:15

It is always so great to see the winner of the Kentucky Derby or the winner of a NASCAR race move into the winner's circle. The feeling one gets for the person on the horse or in the car is a reflection of what one feels about life. When one has the feeling that he or she is a winner in life, then one knows how the person on the horse or in the car is feeling at the time. Every day should be a winning day with the game of life.

When one has a winning attitude, then every day is filled with joy. Recognizing there is enough of everything for everyone at all times brings forth the joy in one's life. When a person keeps the thought of abundance in his or her mind, then there is no room for thoughts of lack to enter the mind. The abundance of the universe is yours when you open up your mind to receive.

All the Father has, which is love, light, life, peace, power, beauty and joy is within each being. The things one needs are always available plus more when one recognizes that the Spirit of God dwells within and is always there for one in time of need. One's needs are always met when the full trust of the Universe is the intention one sets in mind. A winning attitude is one of the keys to a life of joy and abundance.

It is difficult for a person to receive his or her good if they are complainers, groaners, or mopers. Those kind of people are looking for people to feel sorry for them because they feel sorry for themselves. With a winning attitude, one takes charge of his or her life and can change lemons to lemonade when a situation presents itself that is not part of a positive attitude.

There was a time when I would get upset with myself and others because something didn't go as planned. When a situation like that happens now,

I stop and take a look at what is happening and then ask for guidance in prayer which always brings me the answer.

We live in a world focused on the material things we think we have to have, but we are not really of it. I know we take part in outer activities such as finances, possessions, and other material arrangements, and feel we have to be part of that kind of world. The world one creates for themselves is a reflection of one's attitude and the way he or she thinks.

The spiritual world is where it all begins because by putting the Creative Force of the Universe (God) first in all situations, then one is guided as to what to do and how to act on that situation. The joy that comes from allowing the Spirit within to guide one's everyday activities is what brings the peace of mind to the person who recognizes all there is, is God. The material things don't mean much when one allows Spirit within to guide one's activities. When one trusts Spirit, then all the needs are met that makes one's life a joy.

The winning attitude is one of the keys that opens the mind to the spiritual world one creates for themselves. Life is good when one knows there is enough of everything for everyone and that all one's needs are met. Always think of your self as a winner.

And So It Is

Don't Waste Time On Yesterday

It is impossible to measure time; for yesterday is gone and tomorrow has not come, and today is rapidly slipping past.
Ernest Holmes, Science of Mind, pg. 638

There are 86,400 seconds in each day and how one spends those seconds each day builds his or her tomorrow. Yesterday is history and a learning experience that builds one's wisdom as to how to live in the now moment.

There are so many seconds wasted each day where people dwell on what happened yesterday, last week, last month or even last year and beyond. There isn't anything one can do about what happened in the past except learn from that experience and use that knowledge to build a better future by applying that knowledge to the now moment and release the experience from the mind.

One should laugh at themselves for the decisions he or she made that created a "not so good" experience in his or her life and put it in the memory bank of wisdom and not repeat that experience again. I know people who have the same story to tell to anyone who will listen, about what happened to them years ago and it ruined their chance to be successful and live a happy life. It is so sad that a person allows his or her mind to sink to the level that they feel their life is over.

There is so much opportunity available to everyone when the thoughts they have are for success instead of failure. The thought one focuses on, whether good or not so good, is what will manifest in his or her life. To dwell on the past is a waste of time and energy and can only bring into one's experience the same kind of "stuff" one is dwelling on. If you are a person who needs to dwell on something to fulfill your life's purpose, then dwell on the now moment because that is what builds your tomorrows. The good thoughts and seeing the end results of what one wants his or her life to be is a way to bring good into what is to happen tomorrow.

There are three 28,800 second segments in a twenty-four hour period that a person should value as a time to practice the now moments each day. When one allows the Creative Force of the Universe (God) to guide and direct their everyday activities, then the three segments become their now moment. The first segment is to create a way to earn a comfortable living. It may be punching a time clock or having one's own business. The second segment should be spent at creating activities that bring joy to one's life and practice living in the now moment. The now moment today is what brings to one the joy of tomorrow. The third segment is to allow the body to relax, rest and sleep.

When a person schedules his or her time in that order, it becomes very obvious that the change one recognizes is a change for good and creates joy in the daily lives of everyone in the experience. As Ernest Holmes writes in the <u>Science of Mind</u>, "yesterday is gone, tomorrow has not yet come, and the seconds in the now moment are ticking away."

The now moment is what life is all about, so make each second of the now moment a time to bring peace and joy, not only to one's own life, but to everyone in the experience, and the world.

And So It Is

The Anger One Expresses Creates More Anger

And be you kind to one another, tenderhearted,
forgiving one another. Ephesians 4:32

The Apostle Paul, talking to the Ephesians told them that anger was not the way to live, because the anger one has within only attracts more anger into one's life. The same holds true about fear. What one fears most is what appears in one's experience.

There is an old Chinese Proverb that says, "the fire you kindle for your enemy often burns yourself more than him." Anger within yourself toward another person is a good example of what the Chinese Proverb is saying. The other person is unaware of the feeling you have about them so the only person that is hurting is you.

I know people do things without thinking of who it might affect or make angry. The person who gets angry is the person that made the choice to be angry because of the perception he or she made of the situation in their own mind. When something is said or an action taken that offends another person it creates a situation that can lead to some very unpleasant experiences.

We live in a civilized nation where those kinds of things should not happen, but they do. The person who is offended should stop, think about what was really said or done, and forgive the person because they may not be aware that they offended anyone.

Everyone has the same amount of love within them. Some people recognize it more than others and are always expressing that love out to others. The expressing of that love feeling can calm any situation because that is the Creative Force of the Universe (God) in action working through you, as you. There is no room in anyone's mind for love and anger at the same time. Make a choice of what feels best for you and allow the love to flow forward because that makes life a pleasure. When love is expressed out from yourself, then only loving thoughts and action are received in return.

The love within can calm the whole body and one can relax to a good feeling that is healthy not only for the spiritual body within, but also the physical body that we all rely on. The anger within can bring about the "not so good feelings" inside and cause a breakdown of the physical body attracting discomfort and disease.

We are all spiritual beings, having a human experience, so why not feed the spiritual body the spiritual food it needs and the physical body can function trouble free. When the anger is allowed to take over, then the conflicts in everyday activities increase and the joy of life is absent. When love is allowed to flow through one's thoughts and the action taken is from those loving thoughts, then the joy of life and the peace of mind is overwhelming.

The flow of love in one's life is a way to overcome the anger and one need not be concerned about offending anyone. Allow the love of God to guide your everyday life and do not be concerned about anger. Forgive those who have offended you and live your life in peace, joy and love.

And So It Is

Love Will Overcome Evil

Fret not yourself because of evil doers.
Psalm 37:1

I was standing in the kitchen, waiting for the coffee pot light to tell me the coffee was ready, while looking out the window at the backyard. My dog Tyson was checking the back yard to find out how many cats and other animals had been there the night before.

I have a humming bird feeder hanging under the roof of the patio and I enjoy watching the little birds get their nectar each morning. I have two birds that stayed all winter and into this part of this year. They share the feeder and are happy with each other because there are times when they both sit together and drink from the feeder.

This particular morning things were different because a third bird appeared and was very aggressive towards the others. I watched as it chased the others away from the feeder but didn't take a drink because it seemed that all it wanted was to claim ownership of the feeder. As I watched, it reminded me of some of the aggression that all animals use in claiming their territory, including man. I suppose that it is the nature of all animals to do that in order to survive.

Man is no different because, as far back in history as one can check, one can find there has always been fighting among tribes and nations. In the jungles of New Guinea and other unsettled parts of the world, there are conflicts among tribes and one has no idea how many people are hurt or killed. That can be expected in that part of the world, but in the settled part of the world there is no reason for it except for the greed for power.

We are watching things unfold in different parts of the settled world and wonder why it has to be that way. It is the evil that exists that brings birth to conflicts that hurt and kill many innocent people. The terrible things that are happening in the world make one wonder how to deal with them. Ernest Holmes writes, "evil will remain a problem as long as we believe in it." Evil exists because of ignorance, because of not understanding divine law and/or because people choose to disregard God completely.

We should love and forgive those who create evil because they do not recognize that the God of good dwells within and pray that they come to an understanding that God is all there is and is present in every being on this planet. I know it is hard to "turn the other cheek" but that is all part of forgiveness. The love of God that is present in all beings is the greatest power in the Universe. Love heals all wounds and solves all problems when one allows God's Love to guide the actions one takes.

One of the actions is to remember a quote from the book Beyond Appearances, "let us lift our thoughts above appearances of evil and recognize that the darkness of human ignorance must disappear in the light of love." Love is the answer. Love brings peace and joy and harmony to anyone who opens up his or her mind to use love as an everyday guidance.

And So It Is

THE POWER OF LOVE CAN SOLVE EVERY PROBLEM

Be perfect, be of good comfort, be of one mind, live in peace,
and the God of love and peace shall be with you.
II Corinthians 13:11

There are so many ideas of what love is that I don't think I have enough paper in my binder to list them all. I read so many stories where the love of two people is so strong that all the horses in the world could not pull them apart. That kind of love I am talking about is for the first few months of marriage or a relationship. The unconditional love one has for others is not the same as the romantic love we read about in the stories of the nation's best sellers.

Unconditional love comes from the spiritual level that dwells within each being on this planet. Everyone comes into this life's experience here on earth with the same amount of the "God stuff" in them. The people who recognize and use the "God stuff" are the ones who create lives of joy, peace and harmony.

The romantic kind of love is a flash of adrenaline that occurs when people meet and sometimes that romantic love lasts a lifetime and in some instances only a few months. Then it dissolves into a situation that leads to disagreement, disappointment and then an agreement to split and go their separate ways.

I know that when these folks took their vows they recognized God in this joint venture. After a short time, God is left out and is never given an opportunity to help solve some of the problems that caused their split.

The presence of Spirit, that dwells within the center of each being, is the spark that ignites the flame that creates the unconditional love for every living thing on this planet. This unconditional love can carry over into the romantic love that can bond individuals together for a lifetime. There was something that caused the flash of adrenaline in the beginning, so why not nurture the God presence and allow the power of love to bloom and create a life of peace and harmony.

The human race was created to love each other and it all starts with the attitude of gratitude toward all living things and especially human kind. I like what Soren Kierkegaard wrote and I quote, "to love human beings is still the only thing worth living for—without that love, you really do not live."

Love is the answer to all problems and the God of love and peace is always there for one to call on at any time, for any reason, and for any problem he or she faces in the daily activities we call life.

And So It Is

Your Attitude Determines Your Success

Yes, the Almighty shall be your defense, and you shall have plenty of silver. Job 22:25

The success of any person, in whatever endeavor, is determined by one's feelings and attitude toward not only one's self, but to all others in the experience. The feelings one has towards other people is a mirror of the feeling within one's self and can be the key to success or not being successful. When the true feelings are expressed out to others, it is an indication of the self-worth within and is an expression of the Creative Good that dwells at the center of each being.

I know people who are or were very successful in their life and the attitude and feelings they had of themselves and all others could be detected by the way they talked and acted. There was a good energy radiating from these people whether it was a one-on-one or if they were speaking to a group. The feeling of satisfaction within each person in the presence of these people made one want to accept what they had to say and follow their action on solving problems. That is why so many authors writing books on how to be successful say a person should stay in the company of successful people.

To copy someone else is not the way for one's personal success to come to them. Each person is created with all that is needed to be successful. Every individual has to uncover for themselves what they have to do in order to recognize what needs to be done. One may have to release from his or her mind the thoughts of jealousy, resentment, judgment, prejudice, and other thoughts that are negative ; the mind cannot process negative and positive energy at the same time.

The Creative Force of the Universe (God) is always at one's defense when the good of God is expressed through one's thoughts and actions. The successful people I know, and have known, were people who were always happy and lived their life in joy because they wanted everyone to live a life of joy and peace. There never was any jealousy, resentment, judgment or prejudice, in the way they talked or the action they took to solve any problem.

The attitude that one has about life is a good measuring stick of how successful one is going to be in any endeavor. Each being is created into this life experience with the same amount of God potential in them and it is the ones that recognize and allow this God energy to express through them that have a life of love, joy, peace and harmony. God is always there to help, so why not set the inflated ego aside and allow God to direct the life that can bring the success we all deserve. It is God's pleasure to give you the Kingdom, so open yourself up to the good and receive your share of the silver the scripture talks about.

And So It Is

Forgiveness Is The Cure For Self-Hurt

Bless them which persecute you: bless and curse not.
Romans 12:14

There are times when all of us can recall a situation where we got upset with someone for saying something or committing an act that offended us. That person may not have realized that what they said or did was offending anyone. I don't dwell in the past, but I can draw from memory a few times it had happened to me and at the time I became very upset.

That hasn't happened to me for some time now because I see the acts and comments from a different frame of mind. The person who gets upset over a comment or an act by someone is only hurting themselves because the other person did not intend to offend anyone. It is a person's personal perception of the act or comment while adding their own negative energy that creates the anger.

One example, I recall, was in the express checkout line in the local grocery store. I know we have all been behind someone who has too many items in their cart to be in the express checkout. To me it was very upsetting as the express line is just for a limited amount of items and for those who have other things to do and are running short on time. The person with more items is usually having a wonderful day and has no intention of offending anyone. It is the perception of the situation by the next person in line as to how they want to feel about it.

The person next in line could get upset and say something to the person with too many items and ruin not only that person's day but also their own day for expressing the anger they have created in their mind about the situation.

Several things could be considered about why the person was in the express line such as: they didn't realize they were in the wrong line; maybe they didn't see the sign for a limited amount of items; or didn't realize just how many items they had in their cart. No matter what their reason, the person next in line is only hurting themselves by feeling the anger he or she has created over such a trivial matter.

Allowing fear and anger to take over rather than expressing love calls for some true forgiveness work. There is no better time to do some forgiveness work, not only for the person with too many items, but more so for <u>one's self</u> for allowing the anger to build in their mind.

All of the negative thoughts and situations can be erased from the mind with one true forgiveness act and then forget it. With forgiveness we can erase the memories from the mind just like the ultraviolet light can erase all the memory in a microchip. Living in past negative situations only brings more negativity into the present moment.

The time to truly forgive and forget is in the now moment and doing so will attract the beauty of life in one's everyday activities. To live a life of peace, love, and harmony is to allow the presence of the Creative Force of the Universe (God) that dwells within to express through you, as you. This will create the joy of life for you and others.

And So It Is

The Truth Will Always Keep You Free

Thy shall not bear false witness against thy neighbor.
Exodus 20:16

There was a saying, I grew up with, that has made a difference in some of my experiences and that is; "you can't tell a book by its cover." That is so true in a lot of situations and it gets people in trouble with other people and institutions that try to be of service to others. You cannot be something you are not and say things that are not true about others.

I have seen friendships crumble and families dissolve because of false impressions from people trying to be something they are not. I have interviewed people for jobs and it only takes a couple of questions to find out if that person is who they claim to be.

I have always tried to live my life by the Golden Rule, and have always trusted that everyone else is doing the same. I have been fooled a few times, but not for long, because being untruthful can catch up with a person sooner than he or she may think. While talking to a person or when working with a person for awhile, I could pretty well figure what was inside that person's head and heart. It doesn't take long for the truth to come out as to what is going on in a person's life.

While on the job a person could be a joy to work with, but when he got home the family lived in fear because of his temper. It is difficult to tell a book by its cover in a situation like that.

I made friends with a lot of people on the job, but did not make it a practice of getting involved in their life outside the job. Sharing the lunch time with fellow workers was always a good time to pick up on information as to what kind of life they lived when not on the job.

A person who lives a balanced life does not have any wild stories to tell and would always be willing to listen to the problems of others in order to see if he could be of help or service. Those were the kind of people I enjoyed being around and they were the ones I always called on in some of the emergency jobs that we had to do.

Working twenty-six years at outside construction jobs in Ohio was an experience in itself because living by the Golden Rule was as close as I got to going to church. The experience I had of church was while I was growing up and that helped carry me through the "non-church" years.

Twenty years ago I recognized how great life could be by allowing the Creative Force of the Universe (God) to guide and direct my life. I don't have to be concerned by the "cover of the book" anymore because I recognize the good in everyone and pray that they too will discover how great they are by recognizing the God Presence within and allow that Presence to govern their life.

Life is so great with God in charge because that keeps me balanced in mind, body and spirit which creates a life of peace, joy, love, harmony and abundance.

And So It Is

ALLOW THE CREATIVE FORCE TO OVERCOME FEAR

For the Lord is good; His mercy is everlasting;
and His truth endureth to all generations. Psalms 100:5

I see and hear how the whole country is living in fear about the economy. When people live in fear, it only creates more fear and that can be an endless circle leading to total disaster on the family level.

As a nation we shall endure as we always have. I know there are enough positive minded people in this nation to override the fear and negative thinking that can lead to hardship for some of the people. I say some of the people because of their mindset and how much they believe the doom and gloom some of the talking heads of the media want you to believe. There are those who thrive on that kind of low level consciousness and try to pull everyone down to their level of thinking.

We each know what we are capable of when confronted with a situation that is a threat to ourselves or our family. The energy within the financial institutions of our nation is no different than that of a family energy: this is in respect to the positive or negative energy the institution chooses to accept.

Now is the time for everyone to look at their life and see where they can add positive energy instead of falling for the doom and gloom we read and hear about. Now is the time to take the family to the park and enjoy the time together instead of clicking the remote and being infected with the negative energy that drags one down.

One might have to alter spending habits and start using more wisdom as to how one budgets the money. Don't start hoarding and saving for the rougher time that the media wants you to believe. Spend wisely what you need to spend and keep the energy of money circulating. When people stop spending, the flow stops and congestion sets in and that creates fear which in turn creates more congestion and pretty soon everything comes to a standstill.

The energy of money is no different than the other energy that has to keep flowing in order for the abundance of the Universe to keep flowing into each of our lives and into the institutions that provide the services that we all need.

I liked what a brilliant metaphysician named Florence Shinn wrote, "all disease is due to congestion and all healing is due to circulation." That is true with our physical body and also true with the creative energies that surround each person at all times.

When the energies are in motion, a healing is taking place in whatever area needs to be healed. That is why activities outside the home are important because they keep the energies flowing. That is why we cannot stop spending because spending keeps the energy of money flowing and the negative energy of lack, we hear so much about, will be healed and life will continue to flow with love, peace, joy and abundance.

Allow the energy of Spirit to be your guide and see how the fear melts away and the flow of good takes you to a higher level of the love that you are.

And So It Is

The Inside Self Creates the Outside Reality

No man can produce great things who is not thoroughly sincere in dealing with himself. James Russell Lowell

I have read the Self-Reliance lecture by Ralph Waldo Emerson several times and I'm always amazed at the new realization I get from it. This masterpiece by Emerson has inspired many young people to find their talent and pursue it to the fullest. I realize there are those who are wandering through life without the faintest idea of what they want to do or where to find it.

Some of the thoughts Emerson put down on paper the morning before the lecture have been repeated over and over by other lecturers before many groups. That information has turned many lives around and brought out the potential of leaders in the community. Those thoughts were able to help build character and integrity in those who recognized that self-thought is the way to create a life of joy and happiness.

When a person makes his or her decision on the opinion of others, then the power within them is given away and the decision is left floating around in the Universe until the intention is set on a specific thought and held in mind until it manifests.

Some of the quotes by Emerson have been used by notable people who helped shape the society we live in today. People like Henry David Thoreau, Walt Whitman, Oliver Wendell Holmes, Abraham Lincoln, Emily Dickinson and Woodrow Wilson are only a few of the famous people influenced by Emerson's idealism and sincerity.

Until one recognizes that what you think is what you become, then any thought one has will float in the universe until that thought is acted on with conviction. That thought will never manifest or become reality otherwise.

The Law of Attraction plays a big part in the manifestation of thought but it is not a new way of thinking that brings about the realization. It started as far back as Socrates many centuries ago when he said, "yes know thyself" and that was what got him in trouble with his peers and ended in tragedy for him. One can research back in history and find that before Jesus there were people who knew the Spirit of God dwelled within but were unable to teach this until Jesus came along and started his ministry teaching that love and the indwelling presence of God are the source of all our good and it is "the Father within that does the work."

The important message in Emerson's lecture on Self- Reliance is that the inside knowing of yourself is where it all begins and that the abundance of the universe is yours when you recognize and trust that nothing is as sacred as the integrity of your own mind. One of the quotes Emerson made was, "Nothing can bring you peace but yourself." It is the guidance of the Creative Intelligence of the Universe (God) that directs the action taken on the thoughts we get from the Universe, to bring us joy, peace and harmony at all times.

And So It Is

THE INVISIBLE FORCE OF THE UNIVERSE SURROUNDS US

*No man hath seen God at any time. If we love one another,
God dwelleth in us and His love is perfected in us. I John 4:12*

I feel the wind in my face and watch the trees bend and sway as the action of an invisible force demonstrates there is a power in action. I know the wind cannot be seen but is visible in the movement of trees with light breeze and sometimes destruction is brought about by the power of a mighty force that brings down buildings and takes lives.

One might call this the action of the Creative Force of the Universe (God) demonstrating the laws of nature and showing man that the one power of the universe is the only power there is. It isn't an evil power at work because it is the laws of nature bringing to the universe the things that are necessary to keep the planet and the atmosphere in balance with the scheme of things. It keeps the planet productive, responding to what it takes to continually create. I see this as a part of the Creative Intelligence of the Universe (God) demonstrating that the power is always there and that it is what keeps everything in harmony.

The scripture verse says that no man has seen God at any time, but that doesn't mean the Creative Intelligence, that I know as God, is not present at all times. This Presence within is ready to demonstrate what is needed to bring good into all situations for the best and highest good of everyone involved.

It is the invisible power that dwells in the center of our being that Jesus referred to as "the Father within." Many other spiritual teachers refer to it as the Soul or the Intuition that guides the thoughts we receive. The action one takes on these thoughts and ideas come from this indwelling presence. Ralph Waldo Emerson referred to it as the Over Soul, which is all knowing, ever creating and is the power within that creates a life of joy, peace and harmony when one is open to it.

The Creative Force has never talked to anyone nor has it been seen by anyone, but the effects of it is visible in the flowers that bloom, the trees that bear fruit, the wind that blows, the lightening that flashes, the rain that cleans our air and is everywhere present in all the cosmos, throughout the universe. The power that holds the planets in orbit is the same power that dwells within each being on this planet and that power can be used to create a life of joy, peace and harmony by acting on the ideas coming from this power and taking action guided by the intuitive feeling from within.

The feeling one has at the center of his or her being or the soul is this Creative Intelligence (God) expressing through us as us. It is the light within that guides us to a more happy and productive life that creates the joyful life every being experiences that is our divine inheritance.

All beings were created to have a life free of worry, struggle, hardship and the ability to always be free. I see that happening for everyone on this planet because with this Creative Intelligence (God) in charge of everything there can be only total freedom for everyone.

And So It Is

Happiness Is Thinking For One's Self

Happiness is a perfume you cannot pour on others without getting a few drops on yourself. Ralph Waldo Emerson

The observation one has of what is going on in the world is so depressing that people are asking; what has happened to the happiness in life? When one watches the evening news, and takes to heart what the talking head is saying, then one gets caught up in the doom and gloom that is the basis of a good news story.

One very seldom hears about the group that is helping the elders or the group that is raising funds to send a student in the community to a university for advanced studies that would create a person of high standards to represent the community. All of this seems to be part of the past and is no longer acted on by very many.

The lack of happiness has taken root and is growing in all areas of our society. The happiness one has in life starts within each being and is shared with others until there is a group who shares with each other and creates the happiness that fulfills the needs of everyone in the group.

The happiness one is looking for has to start within one's self while building your own little world around you with the happiness you desire. It seems like everyone expects the government to spread the happiness to all corners of the country, and when it doesn't happen the thought of failure by the government is what the talking heads of the news builds their stories on.

There isn't anyone in the world that can make one happy except one's self. The only person that can create happiness is the one who is searching for happiness. It all starts from the center of our being where the Creative Force of the Universe (God) dwells. Jesus referred to it as the Father within and said that it is the Father within that does the work for you in solving problems.

Since it is happiness most people are expecting, then it is

time they do the work on themselves to create the happiness they desire. The God of my understanding is always there ready to do whatever is asked of It in order to find the solution needed to solve whatever the problem may be.

Don't expect anything outside of yourself to create happiness in your life because nobody can create happiness for you. It is how you feel about yourself and your Creator and how you feel toward others that brings to you the love and happiness you desire.

Abraham Lincoln made a statement, "a person is as happy as they make up their minds to be." That is so true because it starts with the mindset one has as to what happiness is. The Local, State, or Federal Government cannot bring happiness into one's life if the person is not open to changing the things in their life to allow the Creative Force of the Universe (God) to create a happy life for them.

It is up to each person as to what to do to be happy because people are different in what makes them happy. The understanding of the spiritual energy dwelling within is the key to turning the lock that has been keeping all the good stuff locked out of one's life and it is up to the person as to when they want to turn the key.

The God of my understanding is there waiting to open the door when the key is turned and will pour the abundance of the Universe into one's life when they are open and willing to follow the direction of the God Thoughts they get. Create your own world of happiness by recognizing the God that dwells within each being on this planet.

And So It Is.

RECOGNIZE THE SPIRIT OF GOD IN ALL OF CREATION

Creation is God making something out of Itself, by becoming the thing He creates. Ernest Holmes, <u>Science of Mind</u>, pg. 582

I get so much joy out of watching the different kinds of birds eating the feed I put out for them. I don't use the bird feeder because only a few could eat at a time. I put the feed on the concrete of my patio and that allows many birds to feed at one time. There are about seven different kinds of birds coming in to feed since I started putting the feed where all of them could eat without fighting over who gets the food.

It is amazing how the birds recognize what could hurt them and what not to be afraid of. If a cat comes around, they all fly away until the cat leaves or until my wonderful dog Tyson goes through the doggy door and chases them away. I have noticed that if Tyson is outside, the birds continue to eat without any fear of him. They know what is harmful and what is not because they rely on the indwelling Spirit for survival.

All of nature is the creation of Spirit and that Spirit expresses through the animals as what man calls instinct. All the animals on the planet have to share space with others: some of them set boundaries and defend their territory, while others live together in harmony and share the food source that is available to them.

There are new discoveries of different species in different parts of the world not of only plants but also of animals. Science has proven that for any kind of animal creation, there had to be the food source first. Without the food being there first, the new creation would not be able to survive on its own. Every plant, animal, bird or fish has within it the knowledge of what is needed to reproduce and how to keep the species at the highest level of perfection. Every plant, animal and bird is created in its own habitat for the species survival and stays in that habitat because that is where the food for survival is at.

One doesn't see a mountain sheep in the middle of a desert or an alligator on the top of a mountain. Everything stays in their own habitat, unless man goes against the way of nature and moves animals into other areas because of an over-population of some species that are destructive to the environ-ment.

I recall when the cattlemen killed off all the wolves and soon were overrun by rodents that destroyed crops and the food not only for man but the other animal species in the area. When man thinks he can go against nature (God) with his egoistic thoughts and ideas, he is in for defeat because the nature of God is to keep every-thing in balance and harmony. The way most over population occurs is because man has tried to implement some ideas that he thinks will better him-self, only to throw things out of balance and create a lot of problems in other areas.

When man can recognize the presence of the Creative Intelligence of the Universe (God) in every living thing on this planet, then the balance of nature is maintained in all areas throughout the whole planet. I know there is a lot to be learned because there are a lot of species yet to be discovered, not only in the rain forests but in the oceans that man knows very little about. By recognizing the Creative Intelligence of the Universe (God) as nature unfolding, then there will be more balance which creates harmony, peace and joy.

And So It Is

Don't Camouflage the Truth of Yourself

The first great discovery that man made was that he could think. Ernest Holmes, <u>Science of Mind,</u> pg. 72

I am a great fan of Alan Cohen because he writes in a way that anyone can understand the subject he is relating to. I was reading his story about the Golden Buddha and the thought came to me about how many people cover their true feelings and don't share with others.

The Golden Buddha was made of tons of pure gold and sat in the gardens of a monastery on top of a hill in Thailand. The monks got word that an army was on its way to take over the community and that meant the army would destroy the Buddha because of the gold. The monks worked very hard covering the Buddha with mud, rocks and mortar to make it look like a stone statue. When the army arrived, the soldiers paid no attention to the statue because it had no value to them.

For several years the army occupied the community and then finally left. All the monks that had camouflaged the Buddha had even left the monastery or had died and no one knew about the Golden Buddha under the cover of stone and mortar. One day a young monk was sitting on the Buddha's knee praying and a chunk of mortar fell off and revealed the gold of the true Buddha.

It is quite a story and relates to so many people who keep their true self covered with something that doesn't allow that true self to shine. I know every being is created with the inner knowing of who and what they are but they don't allow the inner knowing to come out from under the cover they have built around themselves.

I fit into that identity up until the time I got involved with the teaching of the Science of Mind. I had built a shield around myself and did not allow the Creative Force of the Universe (God) to be the best part of my life. I had too many things to do for <u>myself</u> to take the time and recognize how good life could have been by paying attention to my true feelings and acting on the positive thoughts that would have made a big difference in my life.

The Creative Force of the Universe (God) is always at work in every being's life whether they believe it or not. The greatest discovery man ever made was when he found out that he could think and that those thoughts created his life whether it was good or not so good. There are times in every being's life that one gets a wake up event and then recognizes how good life could be by paying attention to the thoughts that were coming to them all along but didn't pay any attention too.

When one wraps themselves in a protective shield and doesn't try to bring the good of the Universe into their life, then they are camouflaging themselves so the truth cannot be revealed. Learn to recognize the thoughts that can bring good into your life and remove the camouflage so the true you can be seen by others who want the same experience.

Positive thoughts bring good things and negative thoughts bring the not so good things. The thoughts one acts on reveal the kind of life one lives. Come out of your camouflage and enjoy a life of positive thoughts that bring about joy and peace and harmony.

And So It Is

THE PROTECTIVE COVER OF GOD IS ALWAYS THERE

The presence of love warms us, the peace of God covers us.
Ernest Holmes, Science of Mind, pg. 560

Last week I wrote about the Golden Buddha that was covered with mortar and stone to look like a statue of stone. The pure gold protected under the cover of the mortar and stone kept the Golden Buddha from being destroyed by the army that took over the area.

This week I would like to expand some more on how so many of us cover the good we are with a protective cover that protects us from unwanted experiences. I know people who would like to express themselves more but refuse to because of what other people would say and think.

Folks, you don't have to satisfy anyone but yourself. The negative thoughts others have are their problems and not yours. The jealousy and resentment they experience are areas that need work on their part in order to get above them. As long as they hang on to that kind of thinking, the good of the Universe cannot enter their life experience.

Every being is created with the same amount of "God Stuff" at the center of their being and those who recognize this "God Stuff" are the ones that live a life of joy and harmony. The Spirit within (God Stuff) will not diminish regardless of how much one tries to cover It up. All beings are created with this beauty of Spirit within and can uncover It at any time by changing the way they think.

One's life is created by the thoughts they think and the action they take on those thoughts. There are people who don't realize how joyful life could be if only they would recognize the Spirit within and act on the good thoughts that come to them. There are those who have covered themselves with the false shield of negative belief about themselves and it will take some serious forgiveness work to remove the shield and get to the beauty within that they were created with.

I had a baffling experience at a local bank Tuesday that left me with mixed feelings about what the problem was. While standing in line, I noticed one of the young tellers who seemed to keep a frown on her face as she conducted business with each person she served. When it was my turn, I walked up to her window and tried to humor her into a smile, but couldn't.

I asked her why she didn't smile and her answer was, "I just don't like to smile." After taking care of my business, she asked if I had a nice long week end, I knew she was trying to change the subject from the comment she made about smiling. I thanked her for asking and then told her I smiled the whole weekend and it was great.

I left without saying anything else so she would have something to think about. To me that was a person who had covered the beauty of herself with so many layers of false protection which could only bring misery to her life. She had no idea how good life could be if only she would recognize the Spirit within and allow Spirit to guide and direct her everyday activities.

When one thinks they need a protective cover, it should be the protective peace cover of God and then they can experience the love and joy of life. The life we have on this planet is too short to waste time on things that do not bring joy, peace, love and harmony into our everyday life.

And So It Is

THE RESISTANCE BLOCKS OUT TRUE REALITY

The Father that dwells within me, He does the work.
John 14:10

Now that the holidays are over and the Superbowl has been played, the groundhog has made his forecast and Valentines Day is over, it is time to get on with life and create the dreams one has put in mind. What does one have to do in order for their dreams to become reality? I have found the best way is to take a look at nature and notice the change around you.

As I go about my daily activities, I see the trees that have lost their leaves and seem to be relaxed and resting. That relaxed time for the trees is very important because they are getting ready for the next cycle of bearing fruit and nuts to add to the abundance we all share in.

While taking a close look at nature, one can begin to understand that the Creative Force of the Universe (God) is always at work doing whatever has to be done in order to keep the Divine Abundance flowing. There is no resistance on the part of the trees or the animals of nature because it is the indwelling presence of the Creator that is guiding the actions they take.

It is amazing that the trees know when to bloom, the animals know when to start preparing for the new cycle of life, and the birds know when to start building their nests. The one common trait in most of nature is that there is no resistance to what is taking place within them.

The failure of most people to live a life of joy, peace, and harmony is when they resist the change they have to make in their life. The ideas that come from the Creative Force of the Universe (God) and the ways and means to support those ideas are met with resistance from man and the dream one has cannot become reality because man gets himself in the way of the flow of good.

The flow of good in our life is always creating a life of joy, peace and harmony when we don't block it with the inflated ego (edging God out) but allowing the Creative Force of the Universe (God) to flow freely and manifest what is needed to keep the Divine Abundance circulating in our life. When one keeps the mind open, ready to accept the good, then there isn't anything one cannot accomplish.

It is the choices one makes that creates the resistance to the good and does not allow the flow to move freely. Man with his choices is the only animal on this planet that doesn't allow the abundance of nature to flow freely; all of the other animals cannot make a choice to stop the flow of good.

Man is the servant of the animal kingdom and one would think man would be the first to allow the flow of good to be the best part of his life. The choices man makes in his own life are what holds him back from the good that flows to all animals in the kingdom because the animal mind of man has become too smart to accept the simple things of life.

If you believe that you are smarter than God, then expect to struggle because you are outside the flow of good. The mind, body and spirit are always in balance when one knows and allows God to guide and direct them to overcome the resistance to the flow of good in their lives.

And So It Is

Always Accept The Best

Delight yourself in the Lord, and the Lord shall give you the desires of your heart. Psalms 37:4

I was enjoying a cup of coffee on my patio, and while sitting there watching the activity of the birds, which included crows and hawks, I noticed a crow trying to break a twig from the huge tree I have in my backyard. I watched as the crow was working very hard for the twig it had chosen. I wanted to get a closer look at what the crow was doing and stepped inside the house to get my binoculars that I keep handy for such occasions.

I know when the animals and birds start preparing for the reproduction of the next generation, they do it with what they have available. I know of no animal or bird that carries a tool belt with everything it needs to do the job with. The crow was using its beak to cut the twig it had chosen. The choice it made was the best for the purpose and it would not settle for second best. It worked very hard and finally the twig came loose from the limb and the crow flew away, only to return a couple of minutes later for more twigs. How many times do we choose second best because the best is too much work or too much trouble to get.

We were created to receive the abundance of the Universe and should not settle for second best when the best is available to us by opening ourselves to receive the best the Universe has to offer. God is all there is and God does not take second place to anything that is offered. I know a dog settles for a bone but would rather have the meat from the bone if it were offered. Its master makes the choice for the dog and only offers it the bone which it accepts. Man is master of the dog and the dog is satisfied with what the master offers.

The Master of the Universe is the Creative Force of the Universe (God) and only offers the best to those who are open to receive. The Creative

Force of the Universe (God) is willing to give man the kingdom when man understands who and what he is in relation to this Creative Intelligence that is everywhere present and is the center of the soul in all living things on this planet.

The crow knew what twig was right for the construction of its nest because it was the Divine Intelligence in the crow expressing. Man is no different when he can get himself out of the way and allow this Intelligence to express through his thoughts and allow the action he takes to bring him only the best the Universe can offer. Your desires are met when you have full trust in this Creative Intelligence I know as God.

And So It Is

The Changes One Makes Creates One's World

Old things are passed away; behold, all things are become new.
II Corinthians 5:17

There are times in my life when I think about the way life was before really recognizing the true meaning of what Jesus said about the Father within. I had heard about the "Father within" while growing up; but no one ever explained to me what it really meant. It wasn't a secret to keep from me, but it was not the way people in that part of the country thought about the God of their understanding.

I have made some major changes in my life since becoming an adult that have created a life and an understanding that is more in line with the way I always thought. My friends and coworkers thought I was crazy when I quit my job, sold my property in Ohio, and moved to California.

While living and working in Ohio the winters seemed to get longer and colder because working construction was all outside work and in all kinds of weather.

I had two brothers living in California and when we talked on the phone during the winter months they told me I should be with them enjoying the warm temperatures. That was probably what tipped the scales for me in deciding to make the move. I do not regret the decision I made because the change is what turned my life in a new direction.

My wife of twenty-five years made her transition four years after we moved to California because of cancer. That was a big change I had to make in my life adjusting to a life that did not include her. I had a very successful business in Fresno that didn't have the same interest for me after she made her transition.

My life wasn't very exciting for about four years until I met my present wife Joanna. Things have changed for both of us because we now have control of what happens in our life because of the trust we have both put in our understanding of what God means to us.

We found the Science of Mind teaching together and it has been a major change in both our lives. It is exciting to have different things manifest in our life by using the Science of Mind principles. Jesus said, "as a man thinks in his heart so is he," which in my understanding means that the Creative Force of the Universe (God) is there for me at all times. It is "the Father within" that does the work to bring what one wants the changes to be. The old thought patterns are taken away and the new becomes the life we were created to live when we accept the guidance of God.

We create the world around us by the way we think and the action we take on the thoughts we get. When one has a desire for something new in his or her life, the presence of the Creative Force within guides us in the right direction when one is open to the guidance. The small world we build around us is a demonstration of the thoughts and the actions we were guided to take on those thoughts to create the changes we desire.

Some of the changes I made in my life before were not so good because I made the choice on my own. Now if there is a choice to be made in my life or the life of others, I always open myself up to accept the ideas that come to me through prayer or meditation. The old things do drop away and the new that replaces them are always for my best and highest good because I listen to the small still voice within. Change is great when one is open to the guidance of "the Father within" because one builds a world full of love, joy, peace and harmony.

And So It Is

THE POWER BEYOND INSTINCT AND INTUITION

The great blessing of the spirit pours through me now,
and protects me in all my ways.
Ernest Holmes, Science of Mind, pg. 257

We live in a universe that is so perfect that most of the people who are aware of this are amazed by the way it all comes together. Everything operates in a perfect way because the Creative Intelligence of the Universe (God) is the energy behind all that takes place. All of creation uses this Intelligence in its everyday activities and it always knows what to do and when to do it.

First time mothers in the animal kingdom know what to do because it is the power of this Intelligence that guides their instincts. The birds that migrate know when to start their flight and know what direction to travel because of this power behind their instinct. The fish in the oceans know when to change locations not only for breeding purposes but they follow the food source that changes its location.

Everything happens for a reason because the Creative Intelligence behind all activity is guiding the energy that everything responds to. The whales in the oceans that change locations don't have compasses or depth gauges to guide them on their way like the man made submarine that has to operate from those kinds of instruments or they would get in big trouble. The same thing with the birds that migrate.

The birds know where they are going because the Creative Intelligence behind their instinct guides them with different signs for them to follow. Some of the signs upon which they rely are the weather, the air currents and the food source. The birds don't need all the sophisticated instruments, like the man made airplanes have, to get to their destination. They rely on the Creative Intelligence of the Universe (God) to guide and take care of their needs from the time they were hatched until the time they expire from this plane of life.

I watched a program on Valley Public Television about the Monarch Butterfly that migrates from Eastern Canada to a place in Mexico each year. I was not surprised, but amazed by the transformation from a worm to a butterfly and how it started its long journey from Canada to Mexico and how it used the warm currents of air to guide and keep it traveling in the right direction. Everything in the Universe operates in perfection because the energy behind it all is the Master Designer (God).

Man does not have instincts like the other animals on this planet: man has intuition. Man has the capability to think and make choices through the intuition that comes from the Creative Energy which is the same Energy that is behind animal instinct. It is the Father within that Jesus referred to that can guide and direct man when he gets his ego out of the way and lets the Creative Intelligence within help him in making choices that will create a better life for himself and all others in his experience.

The thoughts man has and the action he takes are what creates the life he lives. The life one lives is full of joy, peace and harmony when the Creative Intelligence of the Universe (God) guides one's everyday activities. Let go and let God bring to you the joy your life was created to be.

And So It Is

God Will Always Be There

I will pray with my spirit and I will pray with my understanding also. I Corinthians 14:15

There is a lot of controversy about prayer all across this country that makes it difficult for me to understand in what direction this country is heading. Things are a lot different for the children in school now compared to what was happening when I was in school.

I know fifty some years brings on a lot of changes in everything. There was always prayer and the Pledge of Allegiance at the beginning of the school day and all the teachers felt good about telling some of the Bible stories in class.

Most of the activities after school hours began with prayer. Now teachers can lose their jobs by just mentioning the word God. The other part that is confusing to me is that the government body making rules about God are the same ones that begin their sessions with prayer.

The Romans did not want Jesus to teach the people that they were "free to think and do what they wanted to do," so the Romans murdered Jesus.

Seems to me we have some of that kind of "Roman thinking" going on right now and the law makers of this country are going along with the "Roman thinkers." Man was given the ability to think and make choices in order to live a life of non-struggle, non-fear and the ability to create for him or herself a life of joy, peace and harmony.

I know that the man made laws do not affect me in my spiritual growth because that is something no law on this earth can take away from anybody. Each of us is our own law maker when it comes to using the spiritual laws of the Universe.

The Spirit within each of us is the guiding light that brings to us a life of love, peace, joy and harmony and the man made laws cannot affect us unless we buy into that way of thinking.

Looks like our children are going to have to learn at home or in their church if the parents want them to know about God and what God can do to make their life a joy.

It is too bad that Christianity and spiritual awareness is meeting the same challenges in this day and age as it did in the Biblical times. No doubt it will survive like it always has, because it is a divine way of life. We know God is in charge and when we put our full trust in God then nothing can stop an individuals spiritual growth.

It is going to take each of us in our own way to keep God at the front of all our thoughts and involve God in all that we do. God is all there is, so use this power for your own good and the good of the world.

Referring to the verse from I Corinthians — that I will pray with my Spirit (make that connection with God) and I will pray with my understanding also (as Jesus told us, pray knowing it is done unto you as you believe). Put God first in all the decisions you have to make and you will get the right answer as to what to say and do. Let Go - Let God
And So It Is

Judge Not

*Judge not, and you will not be judged; condemn not
and you will not be condemned. Luke 6:37*

I grew up in a part of the country where the fear of God and judgment of others was a way of life. I graduated from high school and was soon drafted into the Army during the Korean conflict. I never did hear anyone call it a war, it was always a conflict or police action.

While in the military, I was exposed to several religions and came to believe that I did not have to fear God and judge others. While growing up at home, I grew up in that kind of mind set and I realize now, as I think back on some of those experiences, that a lot of people were wrongly judged and everyone seemed to put their own label on them. In other words, they were condemned by the very people who were supposed to care for them and help them to provide for their families through employment or their own business. I can see now how wrong it was to even think of passing judgment on someone. "Judge not and you will not be judged" really left an impact on me once I embodied what the true meaning of it meant.

I know, as we live our lives now, we don't have to be concerned about what other people think of us because we don't have to apologize to anyone for what we believe about the God we know and understand. This is America and we are free to believe in what works best for us.

In John 7:24 Jesus said, "Judge not by appearance; but judge with right judgment." When you are judging by appearances, you are judging from your five senses and it is not right for you to do that because you will be judged in return.

Judge with right judgment and you are using your spiritual mind to make your judgment and it is always for the best and highest good of you and everyone involved.

The story about the Prodigal Son in the book of Luke 15:11-32 is a good lesson about judgment and condemning. When the younger son returned home his father welcomed him with open arms. The son asks for forgiveness but the father did not forgive the son because he (the father) never did judge or condemn the son so there was no reason to forgive.

We have to forgive ourselves and others that we feel have wronged us in order to satisfy the Spirit within us. You have to forgive yourself through God because God cannot forgive you because God has never judged or condemned you, so there isn't anything for God to forgive.

When we live our life helping others to recognize who and what they are, then there is no reason for anyone to judge us. Should someone judge us, it would be "right judgment" because it would be through their recognition of the spiritual part of us at work. To live a life of peace and joy, always do unto others as you would have them do unto you.

And So It Is

Create Your Own Calm

And he arose, and rebuked the wind, and said to the sea, peace be still, and the winds ceased, and there was great calm. Mark 4:39

We all know there are four seasons in each year. The people on the East Coast and in the Mid-West have a fifth season. The weather forecasters start early in the Spring to alert people what to expect in the "storm season."

The fear that is generated from these forecasts is a constant worry for the people who live in these areas. I lived in the Mid-West most of my life and I know how much fear people have when there is a lightning storm taking place.

The lightning storms are a must in order to keep the balance of electricity in both the earth and the surrounding atmosphere. The electrons are positive and negative and when there is a build up of one more than the other, then there is a discharge from a cloud to the earth or from the earth to the cloud.

I don't intend to give a lesson in physics, but am just giving the reason for lightning storms. Everything has a season on this planet because it was created in Divine Order, so everything stays balanced.

In Mark 4:36-39 the story is told of how the people with Jesus thought they were doomed by a storm at sea. They woke Jesus and He calmed the storm at sea by commanding "peace be still." The winds stopped, the rough seas calmed and all was well.

How many times do we create a storm in our minds that causes fear, struggle and most of the time causes physical problems. We were not put on this planet to experience fear, struggle and all the other "stuff" that goes along with negative thinking. We are the only animal on this planet that can make a choice of how we want our life to be.

When we allow "the Father within" to guide and direct our choices, then there is no fear or struggle. We create our own calm by the way we think; we know how to not let the storms of our mind create a lot of fear and struggle.

When there is a situation in your life that is causing some fear to creep into your thoughts, the best thing to do is get quiet and repeat "peace be still" until your mind is at ease and the fear thoughts are gone.

It is a lot better than counting to ten and hoping the thoughts go away. It is your choice as to what you want your life to be. Change your thinking to more positive "stuff" and allow the "Father within" to guide your everyday life.

You will soon see that all the storms you created in your mind were so useless, because you now allow the God Power within to calm the mind when a storm is brewing.

Enjoy life as it was meant to be and pass the joy along to others.

And So It Is

MAKE THE RIGHT DECISION THROUGH GOD

One God and Father of all, who is above all, and through all, and in you all. Ephesians 4:6

I was driving back from Bakersfield a couple of weeks ago and the thought kept coming to me about how much the family traditions I grew up with are still part of my life. I know a lot of things have changed since I left home, but the basics of living a good life are still very much valued when it comes to making decisions.

I try to find out as much as I can about what affect a decision would have on me, my family, and above all, the people who would be affected by the decision I made. I know that there are times when people make a decision that creates a lot of problems for them and all others involved because they didn't take time to check it out.

The way we live our lives is most important to us and all others who are affected by the decision we make. Without allowing God to give us the answers our decision is more difficult. I know a lot of things that were handed down by my Grandfather, to my Father, and then on to me, no longer serve me the way they did them.

I don't need my grandfathers horse to pull my buggy because we are all on our own path to living a life of joy, peace and harmony. Some of the "hand me down" ideas are still part of my life when it comes to doing the right thing for myself and others.

I learned right from wrong at a very young age and have always exercised what was handed down to me to make my life good and be good to all others involved. As we continue on our spiritual path, we have to do what is good for us because nobody else can do it for us.

Ephesians 4:23 says "And be renewed by the spirit of the mind," which to me means you have to think for yourself and not allow others to influence the decision you make when it affects your life and the lives of others. Always keep an open mind about whatever you have to make a decision on, and don't make up your mind as to what to do until you have had time to think about it.

There are so many people who make up their minds before the question is ever asked. It is easy to say "yes" or "no" to something before the whole idea is presented. I think that is what happens in different committees when making a decision for the benefit of a group or the whole community. When you get too quick with your answer, sometimes it is very hard to retract, and start over.

A decision that affects you and the others around you should be a decision made after you have had time to think about it and allow the God within to help you with the answer.

Have a happy Life.
And So It Is

A Positive Attitude Is Always Best

Go thyway; and as thou has believed, so be it done unto thee.
Matthew 8:13

I enjoy going to the mall and just sitting and watching people as they hurry from one store to another. I have noticed that most of the people in a big hurry have very serious and determined expressions on their faces. I believe that most of these people have an attitude that they have to do everything themselves if it is to get done.

We might bulldoze our way though life for awhile, but then things seem to pile up around us and we don't know which way to turn or what to do. That is when fear, resentment and anger come into our lives and the attitude we create from those kinds of thoughts and the action we take at that time, are not part of the nature of man God intended.

We were created in the image and likeness of God and that does not include negative thinking or acting. The attitude we create for ourselves reflects the kind of life we live. The person who enjoys life is the person that does not try to do it all by themselves; instead, they allow God to guide and direct them in the decisions they make and the action they take on those decisions.

The energy we receive from other people can make a big difference in our attitude and a difference in what we are doing.

Alan was a young executive with a fast growing company and was asked to do a workshop for some of the employees with the company. Alan had never spoken before a large group and was allowing his fear to interrupt his workshop because he was paying more attention to the people who seemed bored than on the ones that were enjoying the workshop. At the end of the workshop Alan was totally exhausted and the workshop did not have much effect on the ones attending.

The following week Alan was able to do another workshop

for another group and this time he focused on the people with a more positive attitude and the energy in the workshop was very high and everyone accepted and enjoyed the information Alan was giving.

By changing his attention, by focusing on the positive people, his attitude was changed and he was able to overcome the fear. Alan enjoyed doing the workshop because the people responded to his positive attitude. By allowing God to express through him in a positive way, he felt so much better about himself and knew everyone got what they needed from the workshop.

Matthew 8:13 has a lot of meaning because when you change your thinking, you change your life.

And So It Is

WE MAKE OUR OWN WORLD

When we learn to trust the universe, we shall be happy, properous and well. Ernest Holmes, <u>Science of Mind</u>, pg. 33

The world that we recognize is referred to a lot as planet earth. It is the fifth largest planet in our solar system, and the third in distance from the sun, with a diameter of 7,918 miles. It is not "my" world because it belongs to every living thing on it.

Man is supposed to be the steward of this wonderful planet to make sure everything stays in order the way it was created.

There are times when there is some damage; but when left alone, the Creative Force of the Universe (God) puts everything back in order. That is the world that everyone should enjoy, but it is not mine alone.

The country we live in is sometimes referred to as our world, but even that belongs to everyone who lives here. The state we live in is sometimes called our world, but it belongs to everyone. I have heard it said that "the people of California live in their own little world." That is part of the truth about the people in California, but it is not the real world we live in.

The county is not our world because it belongs to everyone who lives here and even the community is not our world because the same holds true for it as the rest of the so called worlds.

The world that we call our own is the world around us. The place where we park our car at night, the place we eat most of our meals, the place where we relax and sleep—that is our own world because we created it.

What you do and have is the world you created for yourself. When a person says "oh he or she lives in a world all of their own," they don't realize it, but they are telling the truth.

We make our own world by the way we think and the action we take on those thoughts. Our world can be good or it can be not so good because the scriptures say "as a man thinketh in his heart, so is he." (Proverbs 23:7). The people who are living in a world that is not so good should look at what they think about and change the not so good thoughts to thoughts that serve them better. The Science of Mind teaching is based on a study that you can change the things in your life by changing the way you think.

Change your thinking, change your life and your own world will be a much better place in which to live.

And So It Is.

Love Takes Away Fear

Blessed are they that keep His testimonies, and that seek Him with the whole heart. Psalm 119:2

Ernest Holmes on fear writes, "Fear is the antithesis of faith. It is the negation of confidence.

Franklin Delano Rossevelt made the statement, "what we must fear most, is fear itself." What he was saying is to not let fear enter your mind when you have a decision to make or when you go about your everyday activities. When you can clear your mind of fear, and replace it with trust in God, your life changes to more peace and joy.

I have worked with people who were afraid to make a decision because they were so negative in all their thoughts; they just knew the worst would happen. I tried to explain to them that thinking positive thoughts could create positive results. What you think is what you get, whether it be good thoughts or not so good thoughts. You create in your life what you focus your thoughts on. A person who can see the good (God's presence) in any situation, will find that only good comes out of whatever the situation is.

When a person can fully trust the Presence of Spirit, to guide and direct them on things that can be life changing, then that person is "seeking Him with the whole heart." When you move one inch toward God, God will move miles toward you.

Seek first the Kingdom, and all else comes with ease, when you get yourself out of the way and let God do for you what you are focused on. The thoughts of fear can block any good that you expect. Try to fully trust Spirit and your life can only get better. Focus on fear and the things you fear happen.

I was at a service station in Porterville getting gas and heard a woman scream as if she were being clubbed. I turned in the direction of the scream and saw this lady in a new Lincoln automobile with the drivers air bag inflated against her face.

I ran over to the car to help her while she was trying to unbuckle the seat belt. The first thing she said when she got out was "I was always afraid this would happen from the first day we bought this car." What had happened was she hit the guard pipe that protects the pumps, with the front bumper and triggered the air bag. A good example of what you think about most is what you get.

I know some of you would say that it would have happened anyway because she hit the guard pipe. You create everything in your life by the thoughts you put in mind, whether they be good or not so good.

I hope by changing your thoughts to good thoughts and having full trust in God, that you prove to yourself that what you think about and what you focus on, is what you get.

And So It Is

Are You A Success?

We cannot demonstrate beyond our ability to mentally embody an idea. Ernest Holmes, <u>Science of Mind</u>, pg. 174

The word success is mentioned only once in the scriptures in Joshua 1:8. "Let only the words of good from this book, come from your mouth, and you will prosper and have success."

Ernest Holmes, in the <u>Science of Mind</u> textbook defines success as the favorable termination of anything attempted.

New World Dictionary says success is a favorable or satisfactory outcome or result.

I think success is when you have reached a goal you set for yourself and can feel deep within yourself the satisfaction of doing what is right for you. I don't think you can truly measure success in each person the same way. Some people feel success is having a lot of material things and other people feel success is peace of mind and a life of harmony.

A person can have all the money they could ever hope for and not be happy. Other people could have very little money but feel very successful because they have as much as they need and live a very happy life.

Mother Teresa attended a gathering with kings, presidents, and statesmen from all over the world. They were there in their crowns, jewels, and silks, and Mother Teresa wore her sari held together with safety pins. One of the noblemen spoke to her of her work with the poorest of the poor in Calcutta. He asked her if she didn't become discouraged because she saw so few successes in her ministry. Mother Teresa answered, "no I do not become discouraged. You see, God has not called me to a ministry of success. He has called me to a ministry of mercy."

There are stories about success, and how it comes about, and usually somebody wants credit for making themselves or somebody else successful because they want to be recognized for what they did. The person who is truly successful is the person who goes about his/her day, with a good attitude, and likes what they are doing.

There are people doing jobs they hate and their attitude shows, they are very unhappy with what they are doing. Those people should go deep within their soul and find out what they would "love to do" and start doing what they would be happy with. I know it is easy to say things like this, but if a person is unhappy with their job, then a change of attitude will make a big difference until they find what they really want to do with their life.

I saw a quote that sure reflects on what I was taught about work when I was growing up on the farm back East. Dad always told us four boys to do the best you can with what you have to work with. When I saw this quote it really drove home what I was taught.

The quote is, "to do a common thing uncommonly well, brings great success." I don't think there is anyone who wouldn't agree. So do the best you can and allow God to guide your life by the decisions you make for yourself and towards others.

Happy Success.

And So It Is

Let's All Take A Stand For Love

Love is divine givingness...Love is spontaneous.
Ernest Holmes, Science of Mind, pg. 43

I know there are a lot of things happening in our wonderful world and it is hard for me to understand the reasons they are happening. In the last fifteen years there have been a lot of changes and most of them are not for the best and highest good of the people involved. We have seen a lot of destruction happen and a lot of lives lost due to natural and unnatural causes.

When the majority of the people on this planet take a stand for love and not anger, then I know the things that are happening will move in line with the Will of God.

Romans 12:2, "Do not imitate the way of this world, but be transformed by the renewing of your mind, that you may discern what is that good and acceptable and perfect will of God." It is the Father's great pleasure to give us the kingdom when we are open to the understanding that God creates out of love and not hate and anger.

Ernest Holmes in the Science of Mind textbook refers to love: Love is the self-givingness of the Spirit through the desire of Life to express Itself in terms of creation. Emerson tells us that love is a synonym for God. We are also told in the New Testament that "He that loveth not, knoweth not God: for God is Love."

Love is free from condemnation, even as it is free from fear. Love is a cosmic force whose sweep is irresistible.

I know that what you set your intention on and focus your mind on, that intention becomes part of your experience. When we can all renew our minds and take a stand for love, then the energy created from that love can change the whole world as more and more people take that stand for love.

I know there are about 450 New Thought churches and centers speaking about and focusing on "taking a stand for love," this week because of

9-11 and other problems that are happening around the world and in this country today. It doesn't take a lot of energy to change your thinking from fear and doubt to thoughts of joy and love toward the people who are having some not to good things happening to them now.

God is love and when you express love to someone you are expressing God toward that person or experience. So allow God to express through you and live a life of peace and joy.

And So It Is

The Beat of Your Own Drum

Our part is to be guided into truth and liberty.
Ernest Holmes, Science of Mind, pg. 272

I was reading a great book by Wayne Dyer called Pulling Your Own Strings. I didn't get too far into it until my mind started drifting to thoughts about allowing other people to dictate what is good for us and what is not good. I know that we can think about a situation in our life where we have all kinds of "help" from other people about how to handle the problems that are causing the situation.

It is amazing to me how other people know what is best for us, and yet their lives are so far out of balance; they can't see that for themselves. When you allow the Creative Force of the Universe (God) to guide and direct your thoughts, then the answers come to you in ways where you don't see any problems at all. There is only one creative mind and that is God's Mind, which we all use each time we have a thought. By living your life through God's Mind, then you don't create situations that cause problems for you or anyone else.

That may be a statement that could be hard for some people to accept, but it is the truth as I see it. God is the only power in the Universe and turning to that power for help is the only way to have a life of joy, peace and love.

We try to solve a problem by ourselves, and before you know it we have created more problems on top of the original problem, and after that comes the headaches, stomach problems, and a life full of worry and fear.

Only you can solve the situations in your life because you were the one that created them. Think about what you were thinking when the situation raised its ugly head and started causing problems in your life. The key to it is what Jesus said in Proverbs 23:7 "as a man thinketh in his heart so is he." What we think about is what we get when we focus on whatever it may be.

By turning everything over to God and allowing God to give us the answers, then we can march through life to the beat of our own drum and don't need the advice from those who know what is best for us. When we get quiet and listen, the answers come to us as a thought, phone call, or a book we pick up. I am not saying it happens as soon as you ask, but keep marching to the beat of your own drum and it happens quicker than you expect.

And So It Is

SMALL BUT MIGHTY

My help cometh from the Lord.
Psalm 121:2

"The presence of Love warms us. The peace of God covers us." Ernest Holmes, <u>Science of Mind</u>.

The creation of all life on this planet expresses the perfection of God in action and the ability of all life to protect itself from danger. As God created each species, there was a way for it to survive as part of the creation. Each species knows what to do and what not to do in order to protect itself from danger.

Man has a built in survival consciousness that he can use when needed to help ward off danger. The trust in God to protect us from danger is a choice we have to make for ourselves.

Captain Eddie Rickenbacker, the World War One "Ace" was considered a great hero. He admitted that through his thoughts it was God he called on many times while on combat missions.

At a minister's conference in Florida, a few years back, one of the guest speakers was Edger Mitchell, the astronaut, and he told the group how he used God Power when he was flying fighter jets in Korea.

He said that many times he would get a "flash thought" to either turn quick or dive quick or even climb quick in order to get out of the way of a missile that was fired at his plane.

He relied on God for the protection that is part of our consciousness when we trust and use it. The built in protection is in every living thing including the birds.

The name of my article is "<u>Small But Mighty</u>" because I found it fascinating how birds protect themselves and their young from the bigger birds that rob their nest of eggs. I have a hummingbird feeder on the patio and there are several hummingbirds that use it. After they get a drink it is hard to follow them because they are so fast.

While sitting on the patio I

noticed a very large hawk sitting in the top of a very high tree in my neighbor's back yard. As I watched the hawk I noticed it kept bobbing its head and almost losing its balance on the small limb it was sitting on. I got my binoculars and soon found out that the hawk was close to a hummingbird's nest and there were several of the hummingbirds diving at the hawk's head. It took about ten minutes for the hawk to decide that it could find food somewhere else rather than being pecked on the head by the hummingbirds.

Even though the hummingbird is the smallest and fastest bird and the hawk was much much bigger, the hummingbirds used the way of protection they were created with and were able to drive the hawk away.

As man continues on his spiritual journey, and allows God to be his guiding source, then the fear can be removed from man's life and we can all enjoy the peace, love and harmony we were created to be. We don't have to be "mighty" like the hummingbird, but make a choice to have trust in the creative force of the universe (God) and allow ourselves to enjoy life on this planet.

With you in Mind.

And So It Is

Pruning Your Tree of Life

Behold, I make all things new.
Revelation 21:5

I enjoy sitting on my patio as the sun is going down, because at that time of the day everything seems to be in harmony with nature. The birds, squirrels, my neighbor's cats and my dog all seem to enjoy the presence of each other. I can feel the energy that is being created at that time of day.

The past couple of months the energy has not felt as strong as before. I finally figured it out, with the help of God, that it was the overgrowth of my shrubs and trees because it seemed like a lot of unnecessary clutter. I started pruning them myself but soon found out that that kind of work was for younger people.

I got the Tribune and turned to the service section in the want ads, and one of the ads lit up my attention. The young man who answered the phone said he could start right away and since then he has done a wonderful job.

As I watched things starting to take shape the thought came to me as to how we could "prune" the clutter out of our minds and lives to bring more peace and harmony. Having trust in God makes life so much more enjoyable because things happen with so much ease.

As I continued to think about what had to be done to the trees and shrubs, I knew it would be a lot of work and that they would look like they would never recover.

I felt a twinge of regret at having had so much done, but there it was. Quickly I reminded myself the pruning was for the good of the bushes and they would come back healthier and more beautiful than ever. I knew that in the spring the transformation would be amazing. Such beauty and abundance of leaves and flowers would prove to me that that is God in action renewing the old.

I thought of the similarity

between the physical pruning of our plants and bushes and the "pruning" we might do in our own life. If we are burdened with any sort of unhappiness, perhaps some pruning is necessary in order to allow a new flowering to occur. If something unpleasant has happened, let us refuse to dwell on it, for if we focus on the negative, we miss giving our best to today. Whatever has happened is in the past and we cannot change it, but we can change our thoughts and choose to live in the now.

Let us start today to prune away our worries and concerns, and make room for a new flowering in our life to occur.

Take the time to prune the clutter of "not so good thoughts and actions" and allow God to express the joy and harmony that you always were and now recognize.

Keep Pruning.

And So It Is

Be In Command of Your Life

He who keeps command shall know no evil thing; and a wise man's heart discerns both time and judgment. Ecclesiastes 8:5

I have known several people who had great fear about making a decision on situations that would affect their life, whether in their home or on the job. They would ask other people for their opinion.

There are times when these people miss out on great opportunities to better themselves, because of their fear of making a decision. These people get passed up when it comes to promotions on the job, or changing something in their own business.

Being aware of that fear is the first step in overcoming it. There are several ways to help yourself, "if" you really want to overcome it. Some people are aware of the fear, but don't want to do anything about it because it would take them out of their comfort zone and they would have to put forth some effort.

Most of these kinds of people are the ones that complain that life isn't fair and that other people get the breaks they should have had. The ones that got the breaks were the ones that had "command" of their life and were able to make decisions that would better themselves and others around them.

These people rely on the positive thoughts they get and the actions they take on those thoughts. The thoughts they get and the actions they take are usually based on decisions they make after listening to that small still voice within (God) and doing what they know is best.

I worked with several heavy equipment mechanics on construction jobs back East, and many were very negative in their thinking and in their solutions to repairing the equipment. If they didn't have everything at their disposal, such as cranes, fork lifts, etc. then the job could not be done in the field and was sent to the shop for repair.

I worked with one mechanic

who, "in his way of thinking," always was able to make the repair, because to him everything was possible when you take time to allow the positive thought to come through. We talked about our feelings about God and he always put God first in everything he did.

I learned a lot from this man and still didn't put it together for myself until several years later. I now recognize that he was in total command of his life because he relied on God for guidance and did not allow fear to enter into any of his thinking.

I have studied the Science of Mind teaching for the past nineteen years and life is great because I have been able to overcome some of the old core beliefs I grew up with that were holding me back from my good. The biggest one holding me back was fear. I have taken command of my life and see only good coming to me and only good outpouring from me because I allow the "Father within" to guide my everyday activities.

Take command of your life and allow the presence of God within to guide you and I know you will overcome the fears and other blocks that are holding you back from enjoying the peace, love and harmony we were meant to experience.

And So It Is

Perception, Perceive, Or Opinion

*But Jesus knew their thoughts and answered, saying to them,
what reason ye in your heart? Luke 5:22*

I know there are times when a situation or problem sticks out its "sometimes ugly head" and calls for my attention to solve it or find the answer. There was a time when I would get upset and angry at other people who were involved in the experience.

Through practice and prayer I have been able to ovecome the feeling that it was someone else that caused the problem. I know that whatever is happening in my life, I have created it through the thoughts and the perceptions I have with what is going on.

After referring to the dictionary as to what the meaning of perception is, I was surprised to find out that perceive and perception are close to the same thing. They both rely on the five senses we were created with—seeing, touch, taste, hearing, and smell. In most cases the five senses through our intuition can bring us the answer to the problem or situation we are facing. In other words, the small still voice within (God) leads us to make the right decision.

Through practice and silence we can get the answers because the awareness of who and what we are leads us to the spiritual uplifting and allows the "Father within" to give us the answer. It is the thoughts we perceive and the perception of the situation that allows us to live a life of love, peace and harmony.

There was a time when I looked for someone else to give me their opinion, so I could make a decision on what to do. The last 18 years have been quite a journey for me, because I no longer allow someone elses opinion to influence my thinking. I have learned that everything I need is within myself and have learned how to use the "Spirit within" to guide my everyday activities. When we allow the opinion of someone else to influence us, then we are giving away the power we were created with that allows us to make the right decision for ourselves.

Through our choices we can be more spiritually realized than ever, for spiritual power does not come accidentally. It comes through devotion, dedication, and the practice of our spiritual skills. I know for myself that what I perceive and the perception of it is always for my best and highest good because I allow the guidance of the "Father within" to give me the answers I need in order to bring into my life the love, peace and harmony we were created to enjoy.

The opinion of others should not influence our decision when it comes to being happy and enjoying life. God's guidance is all you need and complete trust that your highest good is being served.

Enjoy Life.

And So It Is

How to Get It — When You Get It

A man's heart plans his way, but the Lord directs his steps.
Proverbs 16:9

I realize that all through the Bible there are many verses that tell us that God directs our life when we allow it. The teachings of Jesus are the most direct as to how it works; more direct than in any other part of the Bible.

We all know that Jesus said "as a man thinketh in his heart, so is he" and another part of the teachings of Jesus is what he said about the Spirit (God) within. He said "it is not I, but the Father within who doeth the work" and he trusted in the Father (God within) to do the work in all the miracles that his teachings tell us about.

When you pray "pray knowing it is done unto you as you believe." This tells me that what you pray for is what you get, when you truly trust the guidance of the Father within. The Father within that I understand is not one that you make deals with. God is not a horse trader and is always acting for your best and highest good when you truly trust the "small still voice within."

I feel the key to a happy and rewarding life is to be able to give of yourself, with no strings attached, or in other words, don't expect anything in return for what you do, and live your life with unconditional love toward everyone.

If you give expecting something in return, then it will not happen because you are blocking your good by the way you think. I know at our Center we teach "change your thinking and change your life," by always trusting God in all that you do.

There is good for everybody in this life when you allow God to guide and direct your actions on the thoughts you get from the Universe.

When you pray for prosperity, for example, but continue to believe in lack and limitation, then your prayer will not be answered, because you block your good by what you believe.

Decide to accept your good today and pray knowing it is done unto you as you believe, and trust Spirit to bring the good into your life. You get it when you understand what Jesus came to teach us.

And So It Is.

THE NEW BIRTH

Except a man be born again,
he cannot see the Kingdom of God.   John 3:3

I know when things are not going well in my life, that what is happening isn't what I expected, then I know I have to stop and think about what I am thinking about.

There was a time when I accepted that whatever was happening was just part of life and that was the way it was. It took me a long time to come to the realization that it didn't have to be that way.

When Jesus talked about being born again, he was referring to the way you think because we create whatever is happening in our life by the way we think.

I graduated from the university of hard knocks about twenty years ago, and now life is great. I don't have the unexpected things jumping up in my life that take away from the joy that I get out of life now. There are a lot of people attending the university of hard knocks and feeling like I did, that it is all part of life.

After I learned how to change my thinking (born again) to only positive possibility thinking, it seems like the whole world changed. I now see the good in everything and everybody, because I know now there is only good in everything there is.

It takes some time to get to this level of awareness, but it sure is worth the time spent. It takes a lot of reading and attending classes and workshops in order to understand what Jesus came to teach us.

Anyone can change the things in their life when they put forth the effort. It is like trying to win the lottery; you have to buy a ticket. This is something you can start at any time regardless of what is happening in your life now.

Through God all things are possible and as soon as you get started you will find out it comes with so much ease.

When a person makes up their mind and puts forth the effort, they create more peace, joy and happiness in their life. It is what Jesus came to teach us and it starts with being "born again" by changing the way you think.

Change your thinking, change your life.

And So It Is

Giving Thanks for the Harmony

Rejoice evermore. Pray without ceasing. In everything give thanks; for this is the will of God in Christ concerning you.
I Thessalonians 5:16-18

I see, in my many miles of traveling, the abundance that has been created here in this wonderful valley being hauled to the processing centers to be distributed to all parts of the country and the world. When I see the truckloads of different products coming out of the fields, I have to give thanks to the universe for the abundance that it pours into our lives.

I think about what it takes for this to happen each year. Man does his part by having faith when he plants the fields. I know when the fields are prepared there are certain things that have to be done and a certain time to do it.

I see the whole universe as a symphony orchestra with God being the conductor and man being just one of the parts of the orchestra. With God in charge, the whole universe plays in perfect harmony because each part of the orchestra has to do its part.

The sun has to warm the soil, the soil has to be prepared, the seeds have to be planted, the seed has to sprout, the plant grows and blooms, the bees have to do their part, and of course nothing happens without water.

The fruit and nut trees have to have the same as the planted seed crops in order to bring forth their abundance each year. They need the sun, water, bloom, bees and room to spread their limbs to support the abundance they bring forth.

When I see all of this happening I give thanks for understanding that none of this can happen without the Creator of the Universe (God) being in charge of the symphony orchestra that brings all the life on this planet into harmony with one another.

The fact that we know that God is all there is, then we can see and feel the abundance of

God expressing all around us.

When you can join in with the harmony of the Universe you have the feeling of oneness with everything. Your life is in balance with mind, body and spirit and the harmony of the Universe is yours to enjoy and give thanks for.

Give thanks and enjoy the abundance.

And So It Is

BE YOURSELF

I will praise thee; for I am fearfully and wonderfully made.
Psalms 139:14

We live in the greatest time since the creation of man. You may think that all the problem areas of the world make it the worst time. Think of all the good there is in your life now compared to ten years ago.

As time goes on, the goodness of God continues to be expressed through the whole world and is now being recognized by many more people than any time in history. I believe more people today are being true to themselves and it has a ripple effect that connects to others throughout the whole world.

The feeling of love toward all people has a big impact within each person who is expressing that feeling out to the world. It starts with each person and how they feel about themselves and who they are. Each person has their own thoughts and should be able to make decisions that help them to become more in touch with the God presence within.

The love you have for yourself is the first step in recognizing the God presence within. There are many books written about how to get in touch with yourself and how to recognize the God presence that dwells within. The books are great, but until you apply that information to your everyday life and be true to yourself, then you are at a standstill in your progress.

As we move forward on our spiritual journey the information we gather should be put into practice in order to recognize the good in our life.

When you are being yourself and enjoying what you are doing, you should not be concerned about what other people think or what they might say. When we live our life with joy and harmony, that contributes to our happiness, what others think is none of our business. If we are going to be true to ourselves and let our feelings be expressed, then the joy is all ours.

We were created to live a joyful and happy life and what others think is their problem. I know it may sound selfish, but it isn't, because looking out for yourself brings more joy into your life. There are some people who might think the things we do are childish and silly, but that is okay.

I was in the grocery store a couple of days ago and a small child was crying because he didn't get what he wanted. He started throwing a tantrum by jumping up and down and crying very loud. It was drawing a lot of attention from others in the store and what happened was the most wonderful act I have ever witnessed.

The father started jumping up and down like the child and in less than a minute the child stopped crying and started laughing at his father. That was a class act on the father's part and he didn't care what others thought. That is being yourself.

It is a wonderful feeling when we can be ourselves in situations that bring out the true self. The God presence within each of us is what makes life so great when we allow that presence to guide our thoughts and actions. Be true to yourself by being yourself.

And So It Is

The Temple of God

Christ in you, the hope of glory.
Colossians 1:27

I enjoy the programs on public television and I contribute to the local Channel 18 to help keep the programs broadcast into the community. A couple of weeks ago I watched a program about Death Valley. I enjoyed seeing how the different animals and reptiles lived in the extreme heat and how they protected themselves during the day when the temperatures reached 125 degrees plus.

It was amazing how they knew what to do at the different temperature levels. The three toed lizard would vibrate its whole body and bury itself in the sand to protect it from the direct sun.

The animals and reptiles that live in that habitat know their limits and protect themselves from the heat by taking the action they do in order to survive. Then along comes a man with the idea to walk the 100 plus miles across the desert in Death Valley without preparing himself to cope with the extreme temperatures and the other elements of the desert. A search team was sent out to rescue him and after three days they found his body and it was so dehydrated they said it looked like a mummy.

The doctor with the search team was surprised that the ravens had not picked his eyes out and the coyotes had not feasted on his body. The doctor said the temperature was so extreme that the ravens and coyotes had more wisdom than to venture out in those kind of conditions.

Then there was a group that was going to run a race across the desert to see who was the "iron man" of the group. Many started the race but only a few finished because it was too much pain and agony for most of them to withstand. One of the few that finished said it was a great spiritual experience and worth the pain and misery.

I could not see anything spiritual about putting the physical body through that kind of punishment unless he was referring to the handed down false belief that one has to suffer and struggle in order to get forgiveness from God.

The God I recognize and understand is not a God that wants one to suffer and struggle, but to maintain a healthy physical body because it is the temple where the spirit of God dwells. The public television program had a good lesson that evening because it showed the wisdom of the animals and reptiles of the Death Valley Desert knowing their limits and protecting themselves in order to survive.

The wisdom of man with an overinflated ego, and the choices he makes, can get himself into trouble because he is out of his designated environment. The animals of this planet were created with the ability to know what to do in order to survive. Man was created with the same ability, but was given the ability to choose and sometimes the choices are not the best in order to survive.

I know there are those who self-inflict pain, but studies show it is a mental problem and not a spiritual moment. The physical body each of us has is a perfect body that houses the Christ Spirit that Jesus talked about when he said "it is not I but the Father within that does the work."

The scripture "Christ in you, the hope of glory" is saying that when one recognizes the Christ within, then the glory of God is always with you and you can use that God guidance in your everyday activity to enjoy the peace, love, harmony and joy we were created to be.

And So It Is

The Intuitive Voice

Hear instructions, and be wise, and refuse it not.
Proverbs 8:33

There are times when one gets a thought in his or her mind and it seems to never go away. The Creative Force of the Universe (God) has given man the ability to receive messages that contribute to his spiritual growth and also his well-being and the well-being of others. It is called intuition and a person should pay attention when he or she gets thoughts that seem to not go away.

There is a message trying to come through and there should be some kind of action taken. We in Religious Science call it the small still voice within and it can be an answer for a problem or a message of what to do or what not to do. The answers to prayers come to us in so many different ways and should be recognized as Spirit expressing through us and it is for the best and highest good for ourselves and others. Prayers and meditation reveal to us the information one needs when he or she takes action through intuition, or what one might call it the voice within.

I read a story about a part-time deputy sheriff filling in for a full-time deputy who was off for the 4th of July weekend. Don's assignment was the rural area that he had never patrolled before. As Don drove around in his assigned area, his thoughts were drawn to a high mountainside that was not in the area he was assigned to.

As the hours passed Don could not shake the thought that kept coming to him that he needed to go up on that mountain. Everything was quiet and peaceful in his assigned area so he decided to go up the mountain to see why he had this strong feeling of being drawn in that direction.

Traveling on a dirt road that was used to haul timber from the mountain was a new experience for him. The road had been washed out in a couple of places so he had to travel with great care.

When the road made a sharp turn to the left, he came upon an elderly lady lying in the road and she could hardly move. She was conscious and told him her husband was over the edge of the road in the brush.

After calling for help, he did what he could to make them comfortable. When the park rangers got there with the emergency equipment, Don was able to talk to the lady to find out what had happened.

The couple were both in their eighties and had been on their son's dirt bike and hit a washed out place in the road and flipped the bike.

Finding these people and being able to help them was the answer in Don's mind as to why he had this strong feeling about going up on the mountain.

I am not saying one should take action on every thought that comes to mind, but when one has a strong feeling and it won't go away, then check it out. The Spirit within us is the guiding system all of us were created with, so pay attention to your feeling, because it is the small still voice within guiding your activities or giving you the answer to a prayer or meditation.

The Spirit of good that dwells within can take one to places beyond their wildest imagination. Enjoy the love, light, peace, power, beauty and joy that flows through each of us because those are the attributes of God that every being on this planet was created with. The love of God always points the way and it is up to each of us to be open to the guidance of good through the small still voice that is our intuition. Enjoy the journey.

And So It Is

THE LOVE WITHIN

God, I thank Thee, that I am not as other men.
Luke 18:11

I read a story in a book I bought a couple of years ago about a young man who was always helping others in any way he could to make life easier for them. The story was a complete parallel to a person in my home town back East.

This person, Jack, was a neighbor on a farm next to our farm. He was always good in school doing his own work and then helping others with some of the problems they were having difficulty with.

He was not the smartest person in our one room schoolhouse, but just had a way about him that reached out to others he felt he could help. Some of the people in the school did not like him because he was friends with everyone and some of the boys thought he was too friendly with the girls that they liked.

I was quite a bit younger than Jack but tried to follow the pattern he set because he seemed to be happy and always willing to help everyone. After he finished the eighth grade, he did not go on to high school because of the work on the farm and, the high school was too far away and there was no transportation except for horseback.

I was still in school when he was drafted into the military in the early 1940s. There was very little information about him while he was serving his country, until my father read an article in the paper about him. The article said Jack had received a battle field commission for his heroic conduct and his ability to lead his platoon when all the other officers were wounded or killed. The rank of second lieutenant was quite an accomplishment for a farm boy with no experience in that kind of situation.

When Jack returned from the war there was a huge welcoming party and everyone was so proud of him and what he accomplished. When I read the story in the book that triggered my thoughts about Jack, I could understand why these things happen to people who live their life willing to help others.

It seems like when I was growing up few people did anything for anybody unless they were compensated for it in some way. Jack was not a man who tried to convert others to live their life the way he did, but he lived his life by the Golden Rule.

I know the feeling of love is embedded deep in the center of our being and is difficult for some people to express. We were created to serve others and with some people it comes very natural to give and serve.

The Creative Force of the Universe (God) is the power of love that is at the center of our being and is the Christ Spirit that lives within each being on this planet. It is so easy to open up and allow this indwelling spirit to guide and direct our everyday activities and know it is always for our best and highest good.

Jack was a very good example of how God expresses through each being when one recognizes the presence within. The thoughts and the actions one takes on those thoughts are always for our best and highest good when one lets go and lets God guide the way.

Life is wonderful when one recognizes the God presence within and allows that presence to guide his or her every day activities.

And So It Is

Negative Attitude

Go thy way; and as thou hast believed, so be it done unto thee.
Matthew 8:13

While in Fresno a couple of weeks ago for an appointment, I had some time to spare and used it for my morning snack at a small restaurant. It was the first time I had been to this restaurant. I walked in and sat down at a table and it seemed like forever before the waitress came to take my order.

While waiting, I was watching the activity of the people working there and thinking why doesn't someone come to my table because there were not that many people in the restaurant. I did get a little impatient and could feel the anxiety building up within me.

When the waitress finally came to take my order, the welcoming I got from her did not help my feelings much. It was as if she was doing me a favor to come and serve me. While waiting for my order I was thinking about the anxious feeling that was building up inside me. I know everyone has a bad hair day at times in their everyday activities and I guess that day was mine.

While sitting there and thinking about the cold welcoming I got from the waitress, I came to the conclusion that it was my negative feeling that brought on the cold welcoming. The waitress was picking up on the negative energy radiating from the anxious feeling and responded to me the same way.

I don't usually give a negative thought a chance to create the kind of feeling I had that day because I usually replace them with something positive. It was not the waitress being negative and responding the way she did, but it was my negative energy she was picking up on or responding to.

I know the Creative Force of the Universe (God) created every being with the ability to make choices and it was my ego that led to the choice I made that day that just added more negativity to my experience. As I was thinking about what I was thinking about, it became very clear to me that I was the cause of the cold welcoming.

After serving me, the waitress was very nice and cheerful to the other people she was serving and I realized more that it was not her negative attitude but mine.

There are people who live everyday with a negative attitude and that is the reason Matthew wrote the scripture verse about how it is done unto you as you act and believe. To quote Ernest Holmes, from the <u>Science of Mind</u> textbook, "Man, automatically according to law, attracts to himself a correspondence of his inner mental attitude." It is so true that what he or she focuses their thoughts on is what happens or what one gets.

The Law of Attraction is God in action and one can attract the good things in life when one uses a positive attitude in all the thoughts they get and the action on those thoughts. Change your thinking and change your life, let go and let God show you the way.

And So It Is

GUIDANCE

Consider the lillies of the field, they toil not,
they spin not. Matthew 6:28

Norman is a young man with a family and working two jobs in order to provide his family with what he felt they needed. Norman was making payments on two automobiles, a home, and trying to keep up with the everyday expenses.

Norman didn't spend much time with his family because of the second job he felt he had to have in order to live the life he had chosen. It was Norman who made the choice to buy the second car so his wife could take the children to the different activities he had signed them up for.

The son didn't care for the athletic activities and the daughter didn't like the piano lessons or the dance lessons, but Norman felt it was the right thing for each of them to do. Norman was unable to attend any of the activities his children were in except on week ends and that didn't happen too often because most of the activities were on an evening when Norman was working his second job. The life Norman lived could have been a lot different if he would have trusted the inner feelings I'm sure he had at times when making some of the decisions.

Every being on this planet is born with an inner feeling called intuition and it should be the guiding system for one to make the right decision when one pays attention to that feeling.

There are thousands of families in this country that want their families to have what other people have and it causes a lot of problems because they live far above their means. They, like Norman, cannot relax and enjoy life because of the choices they have made in order to "keep up with the Joneses."

The intuition each person is born with is only part of the protective system the Creator of the Universe (God) has equipped the human being with. Man has the ability to think and along with the thinking comes wisdom which should be used in making decisions for one's highest good.

When wisdom is not used, some of the choices that are made can create a hardship on everyone in the experience. With the protective system that man was created with, there is no reason for anyone to experience a hardship when one pays attention to the feeling inside.

It takes trust in those feelings because that is the Creative Force of the Universe (God) in action in you as you. One should always trust that "gut feeling" when there is a choice to be made that affects you and everyone else in the experience. Life on this planet is a joy when one trusts the Universe to guide the thoughts and choices one makes. Like the scripture verse says "The lillies of the field toil not and they spin not" because they are doing what they were created to do and that is just being.

A person does not have to toil and struggle when he or she relies on the "Father within" to help with the decisions that are being made for one's highest good.

Enjoy a life with the love, light, life, peace, power, beauty and joy because that is all part of you and also a part of God. Enjoy life and don't be another Norman.

And So It Is

FRIENDSHIP
A friend loveth at all times.
Proverbs 17:17

I have heard it said so many times in so many situations that "a friend in need is a friend indeed," and didn't really understand the full meaning of that statement until I was reading a book about two people who grew up together. They were always together and taking part in the same activities while in school and also activities they did after school. The bond between them seemed like it could not be broken for any reason, or by anything each was involved in when they were not together.

After finishing school they went their separate ways but kept in contact with each other for several years and then the calls got further and further apart in time. The visits they made to their home town were never at the same time and the relationship seemed to die away completely.

The parents of each man would meet at different functions in their home town and pass information as to how each man was doing.

One of the men was having a health challenge and needed a kidney transplant and no member of his family was a match. Even though the two men had not contacted each other in twenty-one years, the bond and friendship they created in school was still as strong in their minds as ever.

When the other man heard about the need for a kidney transplant and none of his family would match, he took a leave of absence from his job and came home. After running some tests, it turned out that he was a perfect match for his friend and the transplant was performed.

The bond of a true friendship cannot be broken for any reason regardless of the time difference or the situation. Had it been the other way around the end results would have been the same.

Everyone needs friends, someone they can trust and depend on when the chips are down and the need is crucial. In order to have friends, one has to be a friend. When a person raises his or her awareness to a higher level of consciousness and expresses love through their actions, then those people attract other like minded people to them. Dr. Holmes, in the <u>Science of Mind</u> textbook says: "That love is the greatest drawing power on earth."

It is so true that like attracts like whether it is positive or negative. One attracts into his or her life what they focus their thoughts on. The law of attraction works either way, so keep your thoughts on the positive way of life and see how you attract others that you can refer to as friends.

The Creative Force of the Universe (God) knows what to do before the thought ever comes to mind. With trust and love coming to you and expressing out from you, then the word friendship takes on a whole different meaning. Remember to have a friend you must be a friend.

And So It Is

Move Forward

As we therefore have opportunity,
let us do good unto all men. Galatians: 6:10

Now that the great feast of 2007 is a memory and we are still giving thanks everyday for the great life we are living, it is a good indication that each of us is moving forward with life. There are times when we feel that life is at a stand still and we don't realize the good things around us that could lift our consciousness to a higher level and bring the feeling of moving forward back into our thoughts.

Life is good when one lets go of the past and lets the Creative Force of the Universe (God) show the way to a good life. There are so many opportunities presented in the way of creative ideas and the action one takes on those ideas which can create a good life and take one forward to the higher consciousness of joy, peace, and harmony.

I know as the ideas come forward that the action one takes has to take into consideration the feelings of all others involved. When one does good for themselves, it should be of a benefit to others. One does not have to provide a good life for others, but only see how the action one takes might affect others. When the action is good and serves others, then the idea will grow and unfold in divine order.

There are so many people who hold on to past experiences and use those as an excuse as to why his or her life is not filled with joy, peace and harmony. The time comes when one has to release all those experiences that do not serve them and allow themselves to trust the Universe (God) to bring forward the creative ideas that will bring joy, peace and harmony into his or her life. It is such a joy to serve others from a creative idea one has taken action on, and watch it unfold in divine order as the Universe (God) takes care of all the details and brings forth other ideas to add to the joy of the experience.

When Paul, an apostle, was talking to the churches of Galatia, he said *that when one acts on an opportunity, make sure it is for the good of all men.* That was the way to serve back then and it holds true today because it reflects on the Golden Rule.

I know everyone wants a life of joy, peace and harmony and it is possible when he or she lets go of the blocks that are holding them back. Some of those blocks are past experiences, thoughts of fear, lack, and limitations that he or she focuses on each day. When one changes their thinking, they can change their life. Good thoughts bring good things and thoughts of fear, lack and limitation bring into one's life the "not so good things."

The good of God is in all things and the ideas one gets are from God. So, why not let God show you the way when a thought comes to your mind; watch it unfold in divine order. Change your thinking and change your life and move forward.

And So It Is

Let It Go

Be not conformed to this world, but be transformed by the renewing of your mind. Romans 12:2

I have a huge fruitless mulberry tree in my back yard that provides shade for the back side of my house and my patio from the afternoon and evening sun. Not only does it provide shade but is a sanctuary for the different birds that stay in the area.

While watching my dog Tyson from the kitchen window making his rounds in the backyard checking on the different scents of the cats and other animals that had been there during the night, my attention turned to the huge tree.

I had noticed the leaves starting to turn a week or so ago and now they were starting to fall. While watching the leaves fall, it brought to my mind how they had served their purpose and the tree was letting them go. I watched with amazement how Nature continually unfolds in a manner that is always on schedule.

The Creative Intelligence of the Universe (God) is always expressing Itself in such a wonderful way. It builds a trust more strongly within myself that all I have to do is believe and trust Spirit to guide me in my every day activities. The trees and all other life on this planet, through Divine Intelligence, know when and how to do what they do in order to survive.

With God in charge all one has to do is trust and allow the creative thoughts, and the action one takes on those thoughts, to bring a life of joy and harmony.

The tree had to shed the old leaves in order to prepare for the renewed life that is sure to come in the spring. There are those who hold on to the old leaves (negative thoughts) and still expect the new leaves to form and bring joy and harmony into their life.

There are those who hold on to the stories of the past where they were beat down and walked on by someone; the more they tell their story, the more of the same they receive. What one focuses his or her thoughts on is what appears in their experience. It works with negative thoughts, as well as positive thoughts.

When one can focus his or her thoughts on the positive aspects of life, then the not so good things change to the things that bring joy and harmony into one's life. Like the tree, there are things one has to let go of in order for the new to unfold.

As the scripture in Romans says, one does not have to conform to others, but change the way they think in their own minds and allow the life every being was created to live on this planet. We are one with all life on this planet, so why not get with the program and enjoy life as it was intended to be.

All life on this planet unfolds in Divine Order because the Divine Intelligence (God) is in charge. So everything in one's life can be a joy and in harmony when one renews his or her mind and lets go and lets God show the way to a wonderful life.

And So It Is

THE ONE MIND

There is none like thee neither is there any God besides thee.
2 Samuel 7:22

There are times when one word left out or a typo can change the whole meaning of the sentence. The Madera Tribune does a wonderful service to this community and like anything that is put in print, there can be a typo here and there.

Last week, in my article there was a typo which read "his other mind." It should have been "his or her mind." There are not other minds, but one Divine Mind that governs everything in this Universe including our minds. The thoughts one gets comes from the one Divine Mind and the action one takes is guided by instruction one gets from the intuitive feeling, or voice within.

The Creative Force of the Universe (God) is everywhere present at all times and is expressing Itself through every living thing on this planet. That is the way I see God in my life and that is what satisfies the spiritual hunger in me. The most satisfying feeling is to realize I am never alone because I know the presence of Spirit dwells within me and I can call on it for help anytime for any reason.

That is what brings joy and peace in my life and I know I don't have to worry or struggle when something unexpected happens that would disrupt the smooth flow of my life. By using affirmative prayer, like the way Jesus taught us to pray, I can get the answers to whatever is needed to keep my life flowing smooth and allowing the guidance of Spirit to direct and keep me pointed in the right direction.

When I stay balanced in mind, body and Spirit my life is a joy because the Spirit within is always expressing through me and that positive energy keeps my life flowing smooth. There are times when a bump in the road of life occurs and things get out of balance. That is when I stop, think about what I am thinking about, and allow the Spirit within to show me the way to get back in balance. What I think about and see with my mind's eye is what I can manifest in my life when I set my intention and focus my thought on the end results.

In the Science of Mind teaching, we teach that if one changes his or her thinking to more positive thinking, then the things in one's life will become more of a joy and not a worry and struggle. When one recognizes the Spirit within and opens themselves up to the guidance that comes through from the One Mind then his or her life can be joy, peace, love and harmony always expressing.

Change your thinking, change your life, let go and let God.

And So It Is

The Gift We Have

Neglect not the gift that is in thee.
I Timothy 4:14

This is the month that brings a lot of excitement to many children because it is the month for receiving gifts. It makes me wonder if the story about the gifts is understood by the ones receiving them. That is the responsibility of the person who is gifted to be a great parent.

What is being learned by the child is the extension of the gift of being a parent. All mothers on this planet, whether it be animal or human, have the gift of being a parent embodied in their subconscious mind and, by following one's thought instructions knows what it takes to be a good parent. That is the gift the Creative Force of the Universe (God) gave all life in order for that species to survive.

Each being on this planet is created with a special gift or talent in some areas of life. There are artists who paint, design and create sculptures; architects who design buildings and other structures; carpenters, welders, mechanics and the list goes on and accounts for everything that gets done in the activities of life on this planet. The gift each being is created with should be recognized and all efforts should be focused on that gift, because that is the strength of who you are.

There are those who take on so many talents that they are not good at any of them because they have spread themselves too thin. In order to be the best you can be it is important to recognize your God given gift and put your strength and thoughts toward that talent. The things you like to do may not be the gift you were created to do, so put your efforts on what you really "love" to do.

On a scale of zero to ten, one should find the highest score in whatever talent he or she loves and put their efforts and strength toward that talent. That is when one finds the gift they were created with. Once the gift is recognized and effort put forth on that talent, then the Power of the Universe will keep bringing new ideas, and ways to perfect those ideas. When one tries to do multiple talents, it takes away from the talent one was created with.

I have a plaque hanging in my bathroom that I see every day and it reads "what you are is God's gift to you, what you become is your gift to God." We all have a special gift that was created at the time each of us was created and when that gift is recognized and the efforts are put forth in that direction, I know his or her life will change.

There are people who have spent a lifetime searching for the holy grail and don't know for sure what it really is they are looking for. When one finds the gift he or she was created with, I think that might be the holy grail for each of us. Live a life with the gift of love, peace, joy, and harmony and don't neglect the gift you were created to be.

And So It Is

CELEBRATE LIFE

The fruit of Spirit is love, joy and peace.
Galatians 5:22

It is a joy for me to see the programs that are being televised this time of year that do not have foul language and violence. It shows me that there can be programs written and put together that are for the whole family to enjoy.

Most of the programs show how the good of some people can be brought forth and demonstrate how joyful life can be. The advertisements refer to this time of the year as the holiday season when everyone is full of a giving and sharing feeling.

To most people the holiday season is something they look forward to because of the joyful energy created by the thoughts and actions of others around them. I know the beauty of all the lights and decorations can create a feeling of joy and love. I then wonder why it is only the holiday season that creates this kind of a feeling. The other eleven months of the year are just as important as the holiday season when it comes to creating joy and love in one's life and expressing that love out to others.

We celebrate the birth of Jesus as the one who was born on this planet and the one who taught us about love for others as well as ourselves. Living a life as Jesus taught us to live can bring love and joy into our everyday activities. It doesn't have to be a certain time of the year to create that love and joy because everyone is capable of making his or her life full of love and joy.

The spirit that dwells within each being on this planet needs the food of prayer and meditation in order to bring forth the fruits of love, joy and peace. The tree of life, which includes the spirit that lives within, can produce the fruits of love, joy and peace when one recognizes the great gift each of us has been given and allow spirit to express through us as us. One does not have to compare themselves with anyone else, but to celebrate themselves for who and what they are.

We are each an extension of the creative energy of the universe and should celebrate each day for the life that unfolds in a way that keeps us centered in mind, body and spirit. When one can stay balanced in mind, body and spirit then the life one lives can be a celebration each day and not just at a certain time of the year.

The renewing of the mind can be a birth that can be celebrated each day because one is living a life the way the Creative Force of the Universe (God) intended.

Enjoy the fruits of spirit and celebrate who and what you are. Let go and let God express Its good through you each day.

And So It Is

ALLOW YOURSELF THE NEW

Build up yourself anew in the holy spirit by means of prayer.
Jude 1:20

I know it is the time of year when one has thoughts of changing the things in their life that do not serve them as useful anymore. For the past seven years, at our Center, we have had things as they were when we first opened. I could see things that needed to be changed, but it would mean getting out of the comfort of what we were used to.

With the support of the board and the congregation, we have given our Center a complete facelift. The front of our building has been renewed to a more welcoming look along with the new entrance or reception area. The new paint gives a feeling of calm and welcoming energy.

We are putting in place what is needed for a healing arts center along with yoga, reiki, workshops for those who want self-help to improve their health and the way to prepare foods that are more healthy. All of this is part of the renewal from the old to something new that can help many on their path to a healthy life. We are combining all of this with what we have always taught and that is the Science of Mind teaching.

I know that change doesn't come easy but change needs to happen if one is to move forward on their path to a better life. Most people start the new year with new ideas and thoughts only to drop back in the old patterns of what was more comfortable and what they were always used to. In order to bring about change one needs to know "for sure" what one wants, then focus one's thoughts on how life would be when those changes manifest and become part of one's life. When he or she can believe that those changes can happen, and then include those changes in their daily prayers, then the Universe (God) will act on those prayers and the change will take place.

The prayer we use in the Science of Mind teaching is the prayer Jesus taught as part of His teaching. The prayer is an affirmative prayer "knowing it is done unto you as you believe" just as Jesus taught. To make things anew in one's life is to give up some of the habits and patterns one is so used to and replace them with what could serve one's needs for a more joyful life.

We get caught up in the comfort and ease of the way we live and don't want to change because it would mean getting out of the comfort zone we are so used to. That was the way things were at our Center until people started making suggestions on the changes we are making now.

When there is something in one's life that is not serving and making life joyful and peaceful, then it is time to pray for the changes that will bring the peace and joy into one's life. It takes effort and commitment and above all, "focus" on the changes you desire and they are yours.

And So It Is

Ask for Your Abundance

*What things you desire, when you pray, believe that you
receive them, and you shall have them. Mark 11:24*

As the new year is starting to unfold, there are those who want this new year to be more abundant. Most people who are thinking in those ways are trying to think of what they can do to bring more abundance into their life. There are part time jobs, changes of career, starting a home business, selling some of their toys, or taking the wife away from the children and finding a job for her.

There are a lot of options and most people give up and keep on doing what they have always been doing. Change for most people is difficult to accept and they feel it is easier to be satisfied with their life just the way it is.

Making a choice to do something else is a major disruption in their way of life and they feel it is not worth the effort to even start making change. There are others who think and act the opposite and continue to look for something more exciting that can create more abundance in their life.

I believe each being on this planet is created with a special talent and when that talent is being activated the abundance of the universe pours into their life. Some discover that talent at a very young age and some discover it later in life and there are those who never discover it.

Every being born into this experience on earth has a built in guidance system called intuition. It is the small still voice within that most spiritual people refer to. When one gets into the practice of meditation and prayer, then the talent each being was created with is revealed.

I know there are those who say "I will believe it when I see it" and those are the ones that are always dissatisfied with their life. Should they change their thinking and start knowing the truth of themselves, then they would start saying "you will see it when you believe it."

Having belief and complete trust in the creator of the universe (God) is the first step to an abundant life. There is no shortage of abundance in the universe and when a person can truly believe that and have trust that God is the source of all their good, then his or her life will change. God will take care of one's needs and bring to one what they pray for when one prays, "knowing it is done unto you as you believe."

The scripture verse has a lot of meaning and is the truth because the Father wants you to have the Kingdom, so ask and you shall receive. It is knowing within that you deserve all the good the Father has to give. When one is open to receive, then the universe opens up and pours the abundance into one's life.

The abundance of the universe is yours when you are specific about what you want, give thanks, and ask for it in your prayers.

And So It Is

Recognize Your Greatness

If a man thinks himself to be something, when he is nothing, he deceives himself. Galatians 6:3

There are so many things going on in the world today that it is difficult to know what to believe and what not to believe. When one focuses one's attention on negative world affairs letting their own affairs build on these negative thoughts, then one creates in their mind situations that are based on world affairs. The most important person is being overlooked and that is themselves.

All beings that have been born into this experience on earth have entered this experience full of true knowledge of who they are and what their destiny on this planet is to be. As one grows from an infant to adult, the truth of who they are has been reprogrammed to the beliefs of what others have been taught to believe about themselves.

It all starts with the parents, the teachers at school and church or his or her own life experiences. When one focuses his or her energy on something that does not add to their growth or add to their knowing who they are and what their purpose on this planet is, then he or she is doing a disservice to themselves.

There are times in people's lives where a situation leads to a spiritual awakening and they start remembering or learning the truth of who they were when they first entered this earth experience. There are also those people who feel they have overcome all the negative comments and experiences while growing up and have put themselves in a higher level of consciousness and feel they are better than others.

With this way of thinking they are only deceiving themselves because it is their opinion they are trying to get people to believe and it has nothing to do with the truth of themselves. When a person pretends to be something they are not, then he or she keeps digging a deeper hole for themselves and the only way out is to know the truth of themselves.

I have known people who lived in a fantasy world by being something they were not and it created a very disturbing life for them. The scripture verse says it all, and for more information and truth about who one should be, go to Galatians Chapter 6, verses 1-8.

To remember and learn who and what we were when we entered this earth experience, one should let go of all the make-believe thoughts and allow the Creative Force of the Universe (God) to bring one the true thoughts that can add to a life of love, peace and joy. We were reprogrammed as infants by what we were taught and what comments were made about us.

I pray that the parents and teachers see the good in every child and maybe someday a person may not have to reprogram themselves to find the truth of who and what they are. I pray that each being finds the greatness that they are and lives a life full of love, peace, joy and harmony.

And So It Is

THE RIGHT LOCATION

A man's heart devises his ways; but the Lord directs his steps.
Proverbs 16:9

There are times when people get an idea that it would be good for them and their families if they lived in another part of the country. One sees so much on TV about what it is like to live close to Yellowstone National Park or in upper New York close to Niagra Falls or other parts of the country that have places that attract people from all over the world. It is nice to visit all those places, but to live there would be the same feeling as living right here in this beautiful valley.

We have the best of all worlds because if we want snow we can drive to the mountains and have snow. If we want the sandy beaches we drive to the coast and experience a day or two on the beach and play in the ocean. A two hour drive in any direction from this valley and you experience a wonderful get-a-way that people travel thousands of miles to experience. If one likes skiing only, maybe one should move to the north central part of the country.

Soon the everyday life would be just like it was in the original place where one lived. People get used to the everyday surroundings, and wonder what it would be like to live in other parts of the country. God created a place for everyone to feel the joy of life and if one does not get that feeling it may be time to change locations.

I know a fellow that moved from Bangor, Maine to this wonderful valley and settled in Delano just south of Fresno. The lady he met and married lived all her life here in this valley and wanted to travel to Maine to see what that part of the country was like. He was very pleased that she wanted to go and he told her she had never eaten a good potato until she had eaten a potato grown in Maine.

They made the trip and they

were in a restaurant in Bangor, Maine and told the waitress they had traveled a great distance so his wife could taste a Maine potato. The waitress said it was a bad year for the potato crop in Maine but the restaurant was importing a wonderful potato that was better than the Maine potato.

He was very disappointed and asked how could any potato be better than a Maine potato. She told him that it was true and the potatoes were grown in Bakersfield, California. These people had traveled thousands of miles to find the best potato and it was grown twenty miles from where they lived.

We get so used to the surroundings that one doesn't realize how good it is until they travel or talk to other persons from other parts of the country. The grass sometimes looks greener on the other side of the mountain until one travels there or lives there for a while. There is something for everyone on this planet and the sooner one finds that place the sooner one can enjoy what God created for them to enjoy.

I know people who would not be satisfied in any part of the world, because they don't know who they are or what they are looking for. Once a person recognizes the spirit within and pays attention to the inner voice, then any place can be called home.

I realize one's heart may want to search for greener grass, but by listening to the small voice within, the direction one takes is the best for everyone in that experience. The right place to be is the place where one is happy and peaceful.

And So It Is

Nature — The Great Teacher

*Because in His hand are the souls of every living thing,
and the breath of all mankind. Job 12:10*

On my way home a couple of days ago I noticed a flock of geese, in their beautiful V formation, flying north. When I got home and could watch them without having to drive, I noticed two other flocks all honking and heading north. It brought the thought to me that it seemed the time to fly north was premature.

I let my thoughts take me back in time to where my father followed the signs of nature in planting the crops and also the huge family garden which was the source of our winter food. Living on a farm in West Virginia was an experience I would never trade for anything in the world.

I learned through my father how the signs of nature were the divine ideas to follow if one was to have an abundant harvest. My father always used the Farmer's Almanac as a guide to plant the crops on a certain date and when the signs of the Zodiac were in the certain part of the body. There was a lot more to it than I can remember at this time.

We raised all of our food and the whole family of twelve worked to get it canned or preserved so we had plenty all winter long. The only thing that was bought from the store, once a month, was flour, sugar, and maybe spices for certain flavors mom wanted for some of her special dishes.

I know the different signs of nature were messages in advance of what to expect the weather to be. The geese flying north early in the spring meant early warm weather and that the winter cold was over with. I know there were signs in the fall that one could predict what kind and how severe the winter would be.

One of the signs I remember had to do with a worm we knew as a wooly worm. If the black on each end covered its body more than normal, we were going to have a long and cold winter. There were different signs that one looked for in order to prepare for what to expect.

I know the people in Pennsylvania are looking forward to the groundhog coming out of its burrow and not seeing its shadow. If he sees his shadow he goes back in the burrow and they can expect six more weeks of bad weather.

There are numerous signs in other animals that people look for and prepare their life based on what the signs mean. I know the Creator of the Universe (God) is in all living things on this planet and is expressing in different ways through different plants and animals.

I am not saying what we believed about the different signs is true neither am I saying it is not true. I do know we always had a high yield at harvest time, not only in the crops in the field but also in the huge garden that we depended on for our winter food.

The Bible verse says it all and what one believes to be true is true for him. When one has full trust in God (Nature) then life on this planet is a joy and not a struggle. The joy, peace and harmony is yours when you trust and believe.

And So It Is

ALL THINGS ARE PART OF THE DIVINE CREATION
Of Him, and through Him, and to Him, are all things.
Romans 11:36

I enjoyed a program on pubic television last night because some of the creatures they captured on film had never been seen before, it was the first time ever that man realized they existed. It was a program about the abundance of life in the oceans and how creatures survive. Only since the early 1990s have scientists been able to get to the depths where some of the film was shot and see the different creatures and how they survive.

The deeper they descended, the darker it became, and the creatures that lived below a certain depth lived their whole life in total darkness. I was amazed at the different colors of light some of the creatures could generate by activating certain body chemicals not only for protection but also to attract prey for food.

There were some creatures that came up from their very deep environment each night to search for food and then returned to the deep before morning. There was a part of the program about the hot lava that formed what they called chimneys at the very deep part of the ocean and the temperature was 170 degrees. There was life of all kinds living in that hot environment.

While watching this film, and seeing how the different kinds of creatures lived and survived this could have only come from the Creative Intelligence of the Universe (God); I could see no other way for it to have happened.

There are so many things one sees and hears about that one doesn't fully understand how it could be that way or what the purpose is. Scientists have found out that for all of life there has to be food and a way of protection in order for any creature to survive.

Part of the program was about the giant sea turtles and

how they came ashore on a island in the middle of the ocean to lay their eggs and then return back to the ocean until next year. No one has figured out why or how they know when to come ashore on the same island each year, lay their eggs and return to the sea.

There are so many things taking place on the Planet that will never be figured out by man. The mind of man keeps expanding into more and more areas and the knowledge gained is for man's survival. That is all part of the Creative Intelligence of the Universe (God) in It's Divine Plan for the survival of not only man, but all life on this Planet.

There is a lot of buzz throughout the world about <u>The Secret</u> and how it works. <u>The Secret</u> that they refer to has been around since the beginning of time and is now being recognized as the Spiritual Law of Attraction. What one thinks about, with conviction, is what appears in one's life.

The thoughts one sends out into the Universe return to one when the thought is at the forefront of the mind. That is why in the Science of Mind teaching, we teach that when one changes his or her thinking, they can change the things in their life.

Like the creatures of the deep that use a light to attract prey, man can use his mind to attract the things one wants in his or her life. The time is now for people to take a good look at what they think about and only think positive thoughts in order to have a life of love, joy, peace and harmony.

And So It Is

Biography

Jim Fox grew up on a farm in West Virginia. He attended church with his family, took part in church activities and studied the Bible in group classes at Sunday School. He graduated from High School in 1952 in time to be drafted into the military during the Korean Conflict. After two years serving his country Jim worked as a mechanic for twenty-five years in Ohio before moving to California in 1979.

He and his wife Joanna found the Science of Mind teaching in 1986 and attended all the classes the Science of Mind had to offer and, after five years of studies, they became ministers. In 1994 they founded the Spiritual Awareness Center located in Madera, California and celebrated 15 years as a church in September, 2009.